9.11.2.

25.5.21

GW00360627

Please return this book on or before the date shown above. To renew go to www.essex.gov.uk/libraries, ring 0345 603 7628 or go to any Essex library.

Essex County Council

Alana Lentin

———

WHY RACE STILL MATTERS

polity

First published in 2020 by Polity Press

Polity Press
65 Bridge Street
Cambridge CB2 1UR, UK

Polity Press
101 Station Landing
Suite 300
Medford, MA 02155, USA

ISBN-13: 978-1-5095-3570-5
ISBN-13: 978-1-5095-3571-2 (pb)

A catalogue record for this book is available from the British Library.

Library of Congress Cataloging-in-Publication Data
Names: Lentin, Alana, author.
Title: Why race still matters / Alana Lentin.
Description: Cambridge, UK ; Medford, MA : Polity Press, 2020. | Includes
    bibliographical references and index. | Summary: «We can›t claim the end of
    racism until we actually understand what race is really about»-- Provided by
    publisher.
Identifiers: LCCN 2019052404 (print) | LCCN 2019052405 (ebook) | ISBN
    9781509535705 (hardback) | ISBN 9781509535712 (paperback) | ISBN
    9781509535729 (epub)
Subjects: LCSH: Race. | Racism.
Classification: LCC HT1521 .L4126 2020 (print) | LCC HT1521 (ebook) | DDC
    305.8--dc23
LC record available at https://lccn.loc.gov/2019052404
LC ebook record available at https://lccn.loc.gov/2019052405

Typeset in 11 on 13pt Sabon
by Fakenham Prepress Solutions, Fakenham, Norfolk NR21 8NL
Printed and bound in the UK by TJ International Limited.

For further information on Polity, visit our website: politybooks.com

Contents

Acknowledgements

Why Race Still Matters is what you get when you have a trusting editor. My editor at Polity Books, Jonathan Skerrett, approached me at first asking whether I would be interested in contributing a proposal for a book on borders for their 'Debating Race' series. I wrote back telling him that, while I was delighted to have been asked, I did not feel competent enough to write on this subject, but that I could propose something else. Although the book did not find a home in 'Debating Race', Polity agreed to publish it nonetheless, and Jonathan supported me as the book vastly expanded from its original agreed-upon length.

There are many people who helped directly and indirectly in the writing of this book. Some of them I have never met. So, although it may seem strange to do so, I want to start by thanking my fellow antiracist scrollers and 280-character formulators on Twitter. Twitter at times is enraging and it is certainly also a drain on my time. But it is undeniable that, were it not for Twitter, this book would not have taken shape in quite the way it has, especially because sometimes I find living in Australia to be an isolating experience. Twitter helps me feel closer to an international community of race scholars. Knowing what I was writing on, Twitter friends sent me countless examples of the 'not racism' I explore in Chapter 2. I want to thank Michael Richmond in particular, who, as well as publishing an article I wrote on 'Frozen Racism' in the *Occupied Times*, contributed many examples and much food for thought.

The Internet has been important for research in other ways. In particular, I am an avid listener of podcasts, and have learned a lot from *Surviving Society*, *Always Already*, *The Funambulist*, and *About Race with Reni Eddo-Lodge*, on which I was delighted to have been asked to appear in 2018.

I am very grateful to have been invited to speak about aspects of the book in several places, occasions that have helped me to hone it through discussion with colleagues. I first addressed the topic of 'not racism' during a conference in Paris organized by the 'Global Race' project in June 2017, to which I was invited by Patrick Simon and Sarah Mazouz. I was lucky to have been invited to visit the University of Amsterdam in late 2018 as a guest of the anthropologist Amade M'charek, who runs the Race Face ID research project on race and forensics. During my stay there, I was invited by Sarah Bracke and Paul Mepschen to give a talk about the themes I cover in Chapter 3. In February 2018, I was delighted to have been a guest of the inimitable Dottie Morris, Associate Vice President for Institutional Equity and Diversity at Keene State University in New Hampshire, to give a public lecture. Dottie had read about me in Reni Eddo-Lodge's beautiful book *Why I'm No Longer Talking About Race to White People*. Most recently, I attended the 'Mobilizing Blackness' symposium organized by Damani Partridge and Mihir

Acknowledgements

Sharma at the University of Michigan, which was one of the most nourishing scholarly gatherings I have had the pleasure of attending, with a group of almost all Black women scholars. I enjoyed energizing and thought-provoking conversations with Pacific studies scholar Katerina Teaiwa, the African-American anthropologist of whiteness Marian Swanzy-Parker, the Afro-German Black theorist Vanessa Thompson, the Black Finnish scholar of race in the Nordic countries Jasmine Linnea, and Charisse Burden-Stelly, whose brilliant work in the tradition of Black radicalism and communism was a discovery.

I am an enormous fan of libraries, and this book was mainly written in them. I wrote happily in the Sydney University law library during the summer vacation of January 2018, the State Library of New South Wales, and the beautiful new library in Marrickville, where I ran to complete revisions on the manuscript after it opened in late 2019.

I was very lucky to have been invited to the Varuna Writers' House in the Blue Mountains above Sydney. I wrote my third chapter there in a difficult week straight after the horror of the Christchurch terrorist attack, and I was grateful for the silence.

This book, as with all my work, is indebted to the endless practical help and intellectual support I receive from my mother, the fearless antiracist, anti-colonialist, and race scholar Ronit Lentin. Thanks always for your honed commentary and your sharp eyes that find all my strange linguistic formulations and grammatical errors.

The intellectual insight of Gavan Titley, with whom I have been working since 2003, is invaluable. Gavan's own Polity book, *Is Free Speech Racist?*, is *Why Race Still Matters'* sister. It is fair to say that there is a rare word I write that doesn't land in Gavan's inbox, and he

Acknowledgements

is always there with both incisive critique and endless encouragement, both scholarly and political. Stefanie Boulila, whose own book on *Race in Postracial Europe* had just been published, also provided me with precious feedback on Chapter 3. Waqas Tufail read Chapter 4 during his visit to Sydney. The brilliant Critical Muslim Studies scholar Yassir Morsi, whose *Radical Skin, Moderate Masks* is a must-read, is my go-to person for puzzling over race in Australia.

Books don't get written without the help and encouragement of your friends and colleagues. I thank my colleagues in the Cultural and Social Analysis group at Western Sydney University, especially George Morgan. Our little team at the Australian Critical Race and Whiteness Studies Association, Deb Bargallie, Fiona Belcher, Nilmini Fernando, Sherene Idriss, Sharlene Leroy-Dyer, and Oscar Monaghan, became a source of nourishment. I am so excited to be building a community with you. Maria Elena Indelicato deserves a special mention for her energy in building the ACRAWSA blog and for being the best co-editor a person could wish for!

To my friends, those near and far, thanks for hearing me complain. Yael Ohana, whom I have loved like a sister for over forty years, and with whom I pick up where we left off as though a day hadn't passed each time we see each other, thanks for being you. To my local girls, Antoinette, Lana, Leanne, and Lucia, thanks for the drinks, the coffees, and the DMs.

Finally, this book was written at a time that was particularly challenging for my love and life partner, Partho Sen-Gupta. Just as I was settling down to write, Partho's brave and uncompromising third feature film about Islamophobia and white supremacism in Australia, *Slam*, was fighting for a place in the white world of the film festival circuit. As I place the final

Acknowledgements

words on the page, the film has been seen by audiences around Australia and has been met with critical acclaim, proving that, whatever the gatekeepers may say, there *is* a public for the difficult conversations we need to have about race. To your endless love and bravery, Partho, I raise a glass of prosecco!

During this time, our strong and beautiful, original and unstoppable daughter, Noam, grew to become a tween. I know you would have liked me to have spent less time at the library, but you also show me that you understand and believe in me. This book is for you in the hope that race will matter less for you in the future than it unfortunately does today.

Introduction

On 15 March 2019, fifty-one Muslim people, mainly of South Asian or African origin, including several young children, were massacred during Friday prayers by Brenton Tarrant, a white Australian, self-proclaimed 'ecofascist' in Christchurch, Aotearoa (New Zealand). Muslim people close to me responded with grief, shock, rage, but not surprise. White supremacism was suddenly on everyone's lips. The Christchurch massacre has since inspired at least two other lethal terrorist attacks. In El Paso, Texas, on 3 August 2019, twenty-two people were shot by twenty-one-year-old Patrick Crusius. A week later, another twenty-one year old, Philip Manhaus, carried out an attack on the al-Noor Islamic Centre near Oslo, claiming to have been inspired by the Christchurch and El Paso events. In Halle, East Germany, on Yom Kippur (9 October), the holiest day in the Jewish calendar, Stephan B. admitted that 'antisemitic and right-wing extremist beliefs' had inspired him to attack a synagogue, ending up killing two bystanders, neither of whom were Jewish (Deutsche Welle 2019). What links all of these attacks and their perpetrators is the fact that they were motivated by white supremacism and the consequent hatred for Black people, immigrants, Muslims, and Jews. One dangerously racist concept stands out as a key motivator: white genocide, the belief that white people are under threat of forced extinction and that this 'great replacement' has been orchestrated by a multiculturalist plot thrust on an innocent public by a nefarious elite.

This book is not about white supremacist extremism or its conspiracy theories. However, I begin with Christchurch, El Paso, Oslo, and Halle because they sharpen what we are actually talking about when we talk about race. Race matters because the things done in its name have the power to bring about what the Black radical scholar and abolitionist activist Ruth Wilson Gilmore has called 'vulnerability to premature death' (Gilmore 2006: 28).

Extreme racial violence is on the rise, but extremely violent racists do not hold the monopoly in this regard. Certainly, according to a growing number of white supremacists in Europe, North America, and Australasia, we are in the throes of a race war. They are armed and ready to act. However, many more people of colour die, are physically or mentally injured, or suffer in other ways at the hands of the state. 'In the United States, police officers fatally shoot about three people per day on average' (Peeples 2019), 38% of whom are Black (Mapping Police Violence n.d.). Thirty-five Aboriginal people in Australia committed suicide in just three months during 2019, which is also a form of racially inflicted violence (Allam 2019). In 2019 alone, moreover, 681 people died while trying to cross the Mediterranean sea to reach Europe (IOM 2019). Speaking of racial violence makes the power of race to divide human beings into those who deserve life and those whose death is dismissed, or even justified,

Introduction

very clear. Racist ideas, practices, and policies do not always result in violence or death, but they are never very far away. For example, just as the French senate was passing a law at the end of October 2019 to make it illegal for mothers who wear the Muslim hijab to accompany their children on school outings, Claude Sinké, an eighty-four-year-old former far-right *Front national* candidate, shot and grievously injured two people at a mosque in the town of Bayonne (Brigaudeau 2019). In a France rendered hysterical by the spectre of 'Islamization', racist policies and the endless polemics that accompany them have violent consequences.

Given this, it is easy to see why many people would be uncomfortable with the argument this book makes, that race still matters. Race matters to white supremacist terrorists. Race matters to the growing number of public figures and academics, some of whom I discuss in Chapter 1, who believe we need to be realistic about what they see as innate racial differences between groups in the population. Race matters to proponents of extreme 'identitarianism' who are opposed to dialogue and solidarity-building between groups. Because race matters to these groups, many antiracists believe that it should have no place in the lexicon of right-minded people. In contrast, I think that while all of these may be reasons to approach the subject of race with great care, they are not reasons for not talking about race.

My reasons for talking about race are bound up with my own experience as a Jewish woman from the periphery of Europe. I was brought up in an Ireland that was still almost monolithically Catholic, where being Jewish, albeit white, was not as comfortable or hegemonic an experience as it may be for Jews in large cities in the US, for example, where they have more successfully become 'white folks' (Brodkin 1999).

3

Implicitly understanding this distinction from a young age, when I used to sit on the living room carpet for hours browsing a book of photographs about the Holocaust titled *The Yellow Star*, instilled in me an understanding of how race works, although it took me years of study to be able to name it as such. However, this was only a part of my trajectory. Before being brought to Ireland as an infant, I had been born on colonized Palestinian land, the granddaughter of refugees from fascist Romania. Today, as a privileged multiple migrant, having moved from Europe to Australia in 2012, I unwillingly perhaps, but unavoidably nevertheless, participate in the colonization of yet another unceded territory, the Gadigal country in otherwise named Sydney, Australia. This knowledge has provided me with a perspective on race and a commitment to unmasking its colonial roots and routes along with my own complicity in maintaining it through my occupation of a particular location in the racial ordering of the place I am in, as well as the world as it is currently organized. My racialized positioning has allowed me to migrate when so many are denied this right. This has the benefit of giving me insight into how race works across contexts, which is analogous to race itself as a travelling concept. I have lived, studied, and worked in several European countries, as well as Australia and, briefly in 2017, the US. This book thus offers a transnationally informed theorization of why and how race still matters across several locations, and as read in multiple languages. I hope this provides an interesting counterpoint to the North American hegemony within race scholarship that sometimes has a debilitating effect on local theory-building. At the same time, I do not pretend to offer a universal account of race. Rather, my interpretation is grounded in my knowledge and experience, gained in the places I know best and which I have read most about, predominantly the UK, Australia, France, and North America.

Why Race Still Matters departs from a simple question that I have been asking myself for a long time: how do we explain race and oppose the dehumanization and discrimination committed in its name if we do not speak about it? Not speaking about race does not serve those who are targeted by racism. But it does benefit those who are not. Racial logic trades on the idea that there are profound forces that shape fundamental human differences – genetic, geographical, world historical, cultural, and so on – which the layperson cannot understand; a bogus idea that must be exposed. Talking about race does not mean accepting its terms of reference. Like any structure of power – capitalism, class, gender, heterosexualism, or ability – the reason we must speak about race is to attempt to unmask it in order to undo its effects. This is what I hope this book can offer.

But first, what is race? And what is racism? And how are the two linked?

I formulate race as a technology for the management of human difference, the main goal of which is the production, reproduction, and maintenance of white supremacy on both a local and a planetary scale. This definition is indebted to the work of many scholars, first and foremost the late cultural theorist Stuart Hall. For Hall, race is 'one of those major or master concepts (the masculine form is deliberate) that organize the great classificatory systems of difference that operate in human societies. Race, in this sense, is the center-piece of a hierarchical system that produces differences' (S. Hall 2017: 32–3). Hall also offers us an understanding that, although race is about the 'inscription of power on the body', it has no meaning as an actual biological or physical distinction that exists in nature

(2017: 47). Moreover, the biological understanding of race is only one way in which the racial distinction is constructed; geographical, religious, cultural, and, only lastly, biological or genetic explanations of why Europeans theorized that they were superior to, and should therefore dominate, non-Europeans were all used to make of race the 'central term organizing the great classificatory systems of difference in modern human history' (2017: 33). Therefore, as Alexander Weheliye writes, it is more conducive to conceptualize race as a set of what he calls 'racializing assemblages', a series of 'discourses, practices, desires, infrastructures, languages, technologies, sciences, economies, dreams, and cultural artifacts' that, together, ensure the maintenance of political structures and institutions in ways that bar 'non-white subjects' from being considered fully human (Weheliye 2014: 3).

Weheliye's concept of assemblages is in part indebted to Stuart Hall's theorization of race as an articulation, or a series of linkages between different structures of dominance. Therefore, we need to think of other structures of power – capitalism, gender, sexuality, class, and ability – as working through race, and vice versa. As systems that produce oppression, ranking, exclusion, and – to use Gilmore's formulation again – the possibility of 'premature death', these, like race, were produced within specific historical contexts. At a general level, the categorization and ranking of humans into putatively natural groupings along racial, gendered, and classed lines grew in necessity at the start of the modern era, in Europe. As Robin Kelley puts it, in his foreword to Cedric Robinson's book on the evolution and development of racial capitalism, *Black Marxism*, race is 'rooted in premodern European civilization' (Kelley 2000: xiii). However, both race and capitalism, developing together and inextricable from each other, matured within the context of European colonial domination over the majority of the world. Therefore, although with the birth of the modern nation-state in Europe racism and nationalism entered into a reciprocal relationship (Petitjean and Balibar 2015), race as a regime of power is 'colonially constituted', as Barnor Hesse explains (Hesse 2016). What Hesse means by this is that, ultimately, race is about the delineation not only of whites from non-whites, but of the essence of Europeanness from that of non-Europeanness.

Therefore, race is above all else a project of colonial distinction and a system of legitimation to justify oppressive and discriminatory practices. This unfurls internally, within national societies, for example producing eugenicist hierarchies of the 'deserving' and the 'undeserving' poor (Shilliam 2018). Racial logic is also at work in the false idea that there are 'enclaves' or 'ghettoes' of 'self-segregating' migrant communities that disrupt the possibility of social cohesion. It underpins the conspiratorial notion that 'rootless, cosmopolitan elites' are responsible for a negative influence on society, to the detriment of the 'indigenous' inhabitants, as has been argued by Paul Embery, a former fire-fighter on the right wing of the British labour movement, mobilizing old antisemitic tropes (Cartledge 2019). Externally, it plays a role in reproducing narratives of European progress vis-à-vis the supposed poverty, or non-existence, of Indigenous and majority world languages and knowledges. As one philosopher colleague once told me, unironically, 'There are no non-European philosophies!' It creates the notion of developed and developing worlds. It casts the white, the western, and the European – each co-constitutive of each other – as neutral and universal, while everything that cannot be captured by these categories is cast as specific only to the time and place in which it is produced, never serving as a global exemplar.

The central ruse or illusion created by racial logics is that everything in the world has a fixed or natural place. That is why extreme racial regimes like Apartheid, Nazism, or Jim Crow punished 'race-mixing'. However, to fully understand why race continues to have power, even after these systems of rule have been abolished, we must understand why it needed to be legislated for in the first place. Race, having no bearing in reality, had to be invented and needed to be constantly secured. For example, a panoply of mechanisms and practices was needed to pin down the US institution of slavery and to attach an inferior racial status to Black people's bodies, before criminalizing them as a group. These included branding, plantation rules, black codes, identity papers, lantern laws, dress codes, and runaway notices. Simone Browne describes the passage of the lantern laws in seventeenth-century colonial New York city, which ruled that the black body remain illuminated at night (Browne 2015; see also Garcia-Rojas 2016). These laws not only introduced practices of surveillance which Black people remain subjected to today, but they also created and policed 'racial boundaries' that still cohere in the common idea that Black people pose a threat to public and individual safety. How else to explain the practice of reporting Black people to the police for simply existing in spaces it is not deemed they should be in? As found in the coronial inquiry held into the death in police custody of Aboriginal grandmother Tanya Day in September 2019, she had been arrested for 'being unruly' because she had fallen asleep on a train while on her way to visit her pregnant daughter (Human Rights Law Centre 2019). She died alone in the 'lock-up'.

Introduction

Police powers and legislation, such as segregation laws, or, to take the aforementioned much more recent example, the ban on the hijab in French schools, are deemed necessary because race is above all else an idea in search of reassurance (Wolfe 2016). It is on such shaky conceptual ground that it needs to be constantly filled with content, fed like a hungry animal. This is what makes it what Stuart Hall calls a 'sliding signifier'. Its slipperiness makes it difficult to pin down. While we argue about just what defines race or whether this or that event or arrangement can really be racist, race is doing its job of, as Hall put it, sidling 'around the edge of the veranda and climb[ing] back in through the pantry window' (S. Hall 2017: 37). Race continues to matter because it is in a continual process of reinvention.

Despite this, for many it is dangerous to speak about race and better to talk about racism as a set of practices produced by the 'ideology', or what has been referred to as the 'folk idea', of race (Fields et al. 2015; Haider 2018a). However, race is not 'stuck' in the nineteenth century, and, as I discuss in greater detail in Chapter 2, it did not 'end' with the Holocaust, Apartheid, or Jim Crow. I disagree that it is sufficient or possible to talk about racism without explaining the genealogy of race as a system of rule and revealing this process of continual reproduction. I believe that racism is better understood as beliefs, attitudes, ideas, and morals that build on understandings of the world as racially delineated. I explore the evolution of racism, only coined at the end of the nineteenth century, in order to make sense of intra-European racial divisions, predominantly antisemitism, in Chapter 2. My point here it that we need to work with both concepts – race and racism – because they are reliant on each other. I prefer to label my approach to scholarship 'race critical', rather than

9

the more common 'critical race', in recognition of the fact that while we can and should use race analytically, we should also question its terms.

Preferencing racism over race runs a certain risk because, outside of scholarly and activist conversations, racism is used in a very particular way in the public domain to confer a moral judgement. It is now universally understood that to be racist is to have erred morally, as an individual. This is why, as Sara Ahmed has shown (Ahmed 2012), the primary response to accusations of racism is horror and outrage: how dare you call me a racist? And as the Aboriginal rapper Adam Briggs said after Australian football players appeared at a party in blackface, 'People look at me like it's my problem. Like pointing out racism is worse than the act itself. Saying "that's racist" creates more drama than the actual blackface situation' (McCormack 2016).

Racism has been successfully personified as embodied by the bad attitude of ignorant or 'vicious' individuals (Garcia 1999). While, as Lewis Gordon argues, 'bad faith' always plays a role in racism, it is not, the full picture (Gordon 1999). And while we must be careful not to allow an emphasis on the structures, processes, laws, and practices that bring race to life to deny individual responsibility for racist behaviours, the predominant approach to racism which centres on the punishment and ostracization of a minority of individuals 'unlucky' to be 'caught in the act' has been far from sufficient as an approach to ending racial rule. As the late founder of the London Institute of Race Relations, Ambalavaner Sivanadan, said scathingly in the 1980s, the 'racism awareness training' events that became popular in the UK 'removed state and institutional responsibility for racism, instead turning it into a "natural" social phenomenon independent of material conditions, a "white disease"' (Srilangarajah 2018). Racism itself is not a pathology, even if the fervour with which its borders are policed can appear irrational. Racism's apparent unreason plays a role in pushing race as a serious subject to the margins of scholarship. This, as well as the balder fact that there is systemic benefit to be had for maintaining what the philosopher of race Charles Mills calls a structural 'white ignorance' (Mills 2007), contributes to a profound lack of racial literacy in the public sphere. Lani Guinier describes racial literacy as 'an interactive process in which race functions as a tool of diagnosis, feedback, and assessment. [R]acial literacy emphasizes the relationship between race and power ... [and] constantly interrogates the dynamic relationship among race, class, geography, gender, and other explanatory variables' (Guinier 2004: 114–15). Racial literacy pedagogy has the potential to unsettle the 'white comfort' underpinning the dominant approach to racism, which relies on individualized, moral accounts and that sees it as out of the ordinary, extraneous, and excessive to white self-understandings. To cite a student who attended Odette Kelada's racial literacy course at the University of Melbourne, 'Growing up I was never taught to think about my race as something that influenced the opportunities that I got or the way that I was treated, whereas as a white person, that has framed my entire existence' (Wang 2018). However, this kind of opportunity to enhance racial literacy is rare and, with the increasing right-wing backlash against ethnic and gender studies around the Global North, the slight opportunities that do exist risk disappearing if we are not vigilant. As Suhraiya Jivraj argues, in universities, students 'rarely get to hear their lecturers teach or facilitate "safe" classroom discussions about racism, particularly outside of specialist modules. To talk about racism or even (institutional) whiteness has become almost taboo' (Jivraj 2019). And while, as Ali Meghji notes, exciting conversations are happening among radical, Black, and other racialized students about how to 'decolonize the university', these are nonetheless happening within settings that are still undergirded by coloniality and an attendant epistemic hegemony which construes 'provincial' western knowledge as both superior and as universally applicable (Meghji 2019).

Why Race Still Matters should be read not as an appeal, but as an affirmation. Race, Cornel West wrote, simply does matter (West 2017 [1992]). As you read this book, however, you will notice that I am frustrated at how *little* race is said to matter. In fact, when those who face racism speak out, they find themselves policed for 'making it about race', as though they – not the persistence of racial rule – were responsible for their own oppression. As one headline in the French republican magazine *Marianne* screamed: 'Race obsessives on the offensive. They import American political correctness, they infiltrate the universities, clubs and unions, they want to ban art, they want to end universalism' (Girard and Mathoux 2019). This book, then, is a call to notice not just when and how race matters but when, how, and why it is said to be of *no* significance. It is a call to notice that talking about race mattering is so often equated with extremism, even as violence proliferates in the name of an idealized racial purity.

Why Race Still Matters circumnavigates a range of debates in the contemporary politics of race. It is not a textbook, and neither is it a holistic account. Supplementary reading into terms I introduce, such as racial capitalism, white supremacism, or racial rule, will be necessary if, as I hope, I have managed to convince you that we all need more and better racial literacy.

This book is a call to notice not just when and how race matters but when, how, and why it is said to be of *no* significance.

Introduction

Therefore, the book explores trends in the politics of
race that I believe are significant and which I have been
tracking for a number of years.

In Chapter 1, I propose that it is pointless to argue
about race using the terms of the discredited and bogus
concepts of 'racial science'. Efforts to demonstrate that
race is socially constructed and not a biological reality
have largely failed, as can be witnessed in the resurgent
popularity of so-called 'race realism' and the defence
by prominent academics and public figures of eugenic
research in the name of 'academic freedom'. Rather, we
need to theorize race as a political project with ongoing
effects.

Chapter 2 posits that the power to define racism
is taken away from those most affected by it. The
widespread tendency to question what is and is not
racism should be understood as a form of discursive
racist violence. However, while the habit of labelling
obviously racist events as 'not racism' by a defensive
white public is growing, this is not new. Rather, to
understand why there is so much debate about what
can and cannot be called racism, we need to revisit the
history of its evolution as a concept.

In Chapter 3, I argue that on the left as well as on
the right of politics there is a dangerous tendency to
downplay the effects of race by dismissing those who
talk about it as divisive 'identitarians'. The constant
production of outrage about the apparent excesses
of 'identity politics' is having a negative effect on the
possibilities for antiracist solidarity grounded in a race-
critical politics. I explain why we should be sceptical of
the intentions of those who argue that 'making it about
race' is playing into the hands of the right.

The fourth chapter examines the ways in which
the objection to antisemitism has been used as a

proxy for a commitment to antiracism on behalf of all racialized people. Politicians' proclamations against antisemitism draw attention away from the fact that it has always been an elite project. Exclusive responsibility for antisemitism is placed onto minoritized communities, in particular Muslims. Instead, in order to adequately theorize antisemitism today, we need to see it as entangled with Islamophobia. Only this will permit Jews on the left to oppose our manipulation in the service of racism and colonialism, returning us to what the theorist of decolonial Judaism Santiago Slabodsky calls our 'barbarian' roots (Slabodsky 2015).

In conclusion, I revisit the key point made by the book, that understanding how race matters is essential for a fuller understanding of our contemporary lives. I propose that difficult conversations about race are taking place among those whom it affects, and it is the responsibility of everyone to reject defensiveness, and to listen and engage. This is, as Stuart Hall put it, a process and a politics 'without guarantees', one that is all the more important for being so.

My hope is to have successfully argued that, far from anchoring us in pessimism, or a feeling that we are trapped in a history destined to repeat, it is through better understanding of how and why race matters that we can all one day be more free. But I also want you to get angry, because, far from a useless emotion (Lorde 1981), it is anger against the injustice that makes race still matter that will pave the way to that freedom; not a selective anger, but a relational one, an anger that, despite my appeal not to leave race behind just yet, motivates us to seek a day when we can do exactly that.

1

Race beyond Social Construction

Useful though it may once have been for denaturalizing race, the well-worn piety that race is a social construct (with exculpatory quotation marks to prove it) does not get us very far. It simply begs further questions: 'Under what circumstances was (or is) race constructed?'; 'Has race been differently constructed under different circumstances?', and so on.

Patrick Wolfe, 'Race and the Trace of History'
(2011: 274)

In 2017, Meryl Streep presided over the jury of the Berlin Film Festival.[1] During a press conference and in answer to a question from an Egyptian journalist, she remarked,

I don't know very much about, honestly, the Middle East, ... and yet I've played a lot of different people from a lot of different cultures. And the thing I notice is that we're all – I mean there is a core of humanity that travels right through every culture, and after all, we're all from Africa originally, you know? We're all Berliners, we're all Africans, really. (Streep 2016)

Although she denies this, Streep's comments were widely understood to be an explanation for the all-white composition of the film festival jury. 'We're all Africans, really', is a particularly dismissive response to the observation of the structural inequalities that result in all-white conference panels, white-dominated media, the white curriculum, and the overwhelming whiteness of the majority of parliaments in countries whose population is increasingly multiracial.

Speaking clearly about race is difficult, as this episode shows. It always invites multiple and competing readings. Because of its inherent instability, lending itself to myriad interpretations, race is a particularly polyvalent term or, as mentioned in the Introduction, a 'sliding signifier' (S. Hall 2017). The body of knowledge you may be thinking about might be completely different to the political implications I have in mind or separate again from the feeling hearing 'We're all Africans, really', spoken by Meryl Streep might have for another person, a victim of modern-day enslavement in Libya, say. But even the comment itself contains several layers. The article Streep wrote in defence of her remarks emphasized the cultural richness of the Berlin Film Festival, which screens films from around the world. She explained that the comment was made in response to a question about Middle Eastern cinema. So, while it seems strange that what came to Streep's mind was a genetic study about DNA and human evolution, it reveals that talk of race and talk of culture are regularly exchanged in commonsense discourse. The reaching for the standard colourblind response – we are all one, human race – papers over the undeniable fact that no number of films from around the world overcomes the persistence of white domination over the Eurocentric culture industry. It is telling too that the preceding words – 'We're all Berliners' – a repurposing of the words of another American in Berlin, John F. Kennedy, were not seized upon in the same way. We know that we are precisely *not* all Berliners; some of us are being confined in camps on the outer fringes of eastern Europe built to stop too many people from becoming Berliners.

Biological ideas of race never completely disappeared from either scientific or public discourse. However, the more apparent resurgence of racial science, and the link to what its popular proponents call 'race realism', is apparent in genetic science and medicine (Roberts 2012) and in the development of technologies of security and surveillance for the control both of 'unruly' racialized groups (Vitale and Jefferson 2016) and of migrants and asylum seekers at the highly policed borders of the Global North (Andersson 2016). It is also a powerful narrative that propels the white supremacist right forward, attaching itself to the conspiracies of 'white genocide' and 'great replacement' that construe ethnonational populations as organically weakened by culturally inferior imposters, most prominently today Muslims (Camus 2015). Brenton Tarrant, the white supremacist terrorist who murdered fifty-one Muslim worshippers in Christchurch in March 2019, wrote a manifesto entitled 'The Great Replacement' in which he interviewed himself on the motives for the attack: 'Was the attack anti-immigration in origin? Yes, beyond all doubt, anti-immigration, anti-ethnic replacement and anti-cultural replacement.'

In this chapter, I make the case that the current terms available in the public sphere to discuss race are not fit for purpose. As I stated in the Introduction, racial literacy is not a feature of western educational systems, whose remit is largely to recreate the Eurocentric nation-state in its own image. Race and racism, therefore, remain

The current terms available in the public sphere to discuss race are not fit for purpose.

special interest subjects. We are not, then, equipped with the tools necessary for challenging racial pseudoscience discourse. For example, there was barely a murmur when, in October 2019, Australian Home Affairs Minister Peter Dutton proposed that DNA testing is required to verify the Australian citizenship claims of women currently trapped in Syria after the fall of the Islamic State (SBS 2019). Of course, there is no link between DNA and citizenship, yet what Dutton's statement reveals is that it is easy to conflate the two because both are commonly understood to be 'about race'.

In the next chapter, I discuss the relationship between racial structures and racist practices such as violence, discrimination, and exclusion in greater detail. For now, I suggest that the failure to connect racism to race as a regime of power allows singular definitions of race as biological categories to define public conversations. Because of the failure to unearth the many cross-cutting functions of race as a regime of power, we have come to see eighteenth- and nineteenth-century pseudoscientific racial classifications as synonymous with race in general. This has two consequences which are relevant to our discussion here. First, we have been unable to interrogate how race is assembled from a multiplicity of rationales, including the geographical, the religious, the cultural, the visual, and the biological, all of which intersect with other regimes of power, most significantly gender. Second, this has paradoxically allowed a biological understanding of race to be retained, particularly within scientific and medical discourses, with a flow-on effect on everyday ways of understanding and talking about human difference.

One of the most serious problems for us today is that what I have referred to as the 'silence about race' has allowed biological race, in a similar fashion to gender determinism, to become a currency on the 'marketplace of ideas' (A. Lentin 2008). Though it never left, with the renewed élan of white supremacy, race seems to have found new wings in these 'post-postracial' times, well after the waning of the racial optimism of the early years of the Obama era. In the rest of this chapter, I explore the context in which ideas of racial science are resurgent. I argue that we must find ways of countering them that go beyond what I shall suggest is the insufficient proposition that race is a social construct that has no basis in scientific fact. This is a truism that only takes us so far, and which risks misappropriation by those with anything but antiracist intentions. I query how we can retain the conceptual utility of race as something that is necessary to understand in the aim of achieving better historical, political, and sociological literacy, while rejecting the false premises of racial science. These inquiries might help us makes sense of the persistent political and social impact that race continues to have.

Eugenics redux

In May 2018, the *Monash Bioethics Review* published an article by a University of San Diego assistant professor of philosophy, Jonathan Anomaly, titled 'Defending Eugenics', in which he argues that 'future people would be better off if people with heritable traits that we value had a greater proportion of children' (Anomaly 2018: 25). Anomaly attempts to avoid the charge of racism by arguing that the virtues of eugenics should not be obscured by the ends to which these ideas were put by the Nazis. However, it is impossible to dissociate an idea from the context in which it emerged and the practices to which it led.[2] The article came to my

21

notice via a tweet from author and academic Sunny Singh on 12 November that year, the same day as the announcement of a new academic journal, the *Journal of Controversial Ideas*, founded under the editorship of Peter Singer, Jeff McMahan, and Francesca Minerva, which would allow academics to publish controversial ideas pseudonymously. Peter Singer, the Australian utilitarian bioethicist well known for his support for animal liberation, is also on the editorial board of the *Monash Bioethics Review*. It is not irrelevant that Singer has expressed disturbing views on race (Grey and Cleffie 2015). In an interview with the African-American philosopher George Yancy, he compared what he calls 'speciesism' to chattel-slavery, and argued that racism is mainly a past phenomenon and that discrimination against animals is more insidious (Yancy 2015).

During a BBC Radio 4 documentary, *University Unchallenged*, about so-called 'viewpoint diversity' in academia, co-editor Jeff McMahan, a professor of moral philosophy at Oxford, explained the need for the journal was due to 'greater inhibition on university campuses about taking certain positions for fear of what will happen' (Rosenbaum 2018). The complaint about the lack of diversity of perspective on university campuses has become 'a central trope of the disingenuous both-sidesism' of those who argue that too much concern with racism, sexism, or queerphobia is propelling a crisis of academic free speech (Mitchell 2018). According to those who bemoan a lack of 'viewpoint diversity', conservative or right-wing ideas are stifled by what they see as the overwhelming dominance of 'liberal' perspectives among teaching and administrative staff at UK and US colleges. According to one 'conservative-leaning professor', this liberal dominance hinders student learning and 'threatens the free and open exchange of ideas' (Abrams 2018). In fact, there are many attacks on academic free speech, but in the main they do not come from 'liberals'. For example, Murdoch University in Western Australia took a case against one of its academics for blowing the whistle on the treatment of international students in 2019 (Knaus 2019).

Jonathan Anomaly also couches his article in these 'viewpoint diversity' terms, a frame in which racial ideas are presented as purportedly neutral, and just another topic of debate (Reiheld 2018). Proponents of such theories calls themselves 'race realists', and argue that there is nothing nefarious in research that finds that different groups in the population can be genetically ranked on a range of indices. The recent emboldening of the 'race realists' should not lead us to ignore the fact that, despite consensus within the international community that 'current biological knowledge does not permit us to impute cultural achievements to differences in genetic potential' (UNESCO 1968: 270), the use of racial taxonomy in biology and medicine has never stopped (Carter 2007; Fields and Fields 2012). Eugenicist ideas and practices did not completely exit the mainstream despite being disavowed after the Nazi Holocaust.[3] For example, the 1994 book *The Bell Curve*, which argued that Black people have low IQ, has had enormous influence (Roberts 2015).

The book's co-author, Charles Murray, is often claimed to be silenced, particularly following the 2017 protests against him at Middlebury College (Reilly 2017). However, Murray is in fact 'ensconced at the center of the conservative policy establishment as an emeritus scholar at the American Enterprise Institute. In 2016, he won the Bradley Prize, a prestigious conservative award that carries a $250,000 stipend. He regularly publishes op-eds in the *Wall Street Journal*' (Yglesias 2018).

Nevertheless, an important key to understanding today's circulation and proliferation of nineteenth-century ideas about the purported genetic inferiority of people racialized as non-white is that their propo-nents are presented as brave, clamouring to be heard above the din of antiracist orthodoxy. It is of little surprise, then, that Jonathan Anomaly is also a frequent contributor to the right-libertarian *Quillette*, an online magazine edited by 'Mistress of the Intellectual Dark Web' Australian Claire Lehmann (Dale 2018). Lehmann herself has defended behavioural genetics, claiming that 'it is measured by IQ testing, is genetically based, and correlates with success in life' (Hochschild 2019). In one of his *Quillette* articles, Anomaly argues that 'good' science is often refuted on moral rather than scientific grounds (Anomaly 2017). Referring to proponents of the link between race and IQ, Edmund Wilson and Arthur Jensen's argument that, as Anomaly puts it, 'different racial groups probably have different cognitive propen-sities and capacities', he claims that 'they were harshly denounced, typically on moral grounds rather than on the scientific merit of their arguments. Their careers were threatened, and people who might otherwise pursue this research or publicly explain the evidence for these hypotheses learned to keep their mouths shut.' Without irony, Anomaly is arguing that 'best available evidence' on what he calls 'politically contentious scien-tific topics' is refuted because of 'the career-advancing opportunities open to those who *symbolically* reject sexism and racism' (original emphasis). However, there is no evaluation of this evidence against the wider literature because, despite its claim to rigour, *Quillette*'s offerings are rather more hyperbolic than they are evidence-based.

It is vital to loudly oppose the notion that eugenics can ever constitute desirable public policy proposals, even those associated with what Anomaly calls 'liberal eugenics', which apparently 'places more weight on individual liberty and less confidence in the wisdom of state agents than early manifestations of eugenics did' (Anomaly 2018: 30; see also Agar 2004). It is also crucial to cast doubt on the proposition that these types of ideas have been marginalized. However, it is insufficient to argue against the contentions made by 'race realists' on scientific grounds alone. To do so is to misconstrue the terms of the race project, which were never purely scientific, but inherently political, and which actually predate the invention of racial science in the nineteenth century (S. Hall 2017). A case in point is science writer Nicholas Wade's response to the 139 geneticists who signed an open letter condemning his 2014 book *A Troublesome Inheritance*. The book rehashes the main precepts of racial science, 'that the notion of "race" corresponds to profound biological differences among groups of humans; that human brains evolved differently from race to race; and that this is supported by different racial averages in IQ scores' (Evans 2018). The geneticists who signed the letter claimed unequivocally that,

> Wade juxtaposes an incomplete and inaccurate account of our research on human genetic differences with speculation that recent natural selection has led to worldwide differences in IQ test results, political institutions and economic development. We reject Wade's implication that our findings substantiate his guesswork. They do not. We are in full agreement that there is no support from the field of population genetics for Wade's conjectures.[4]

However, this was immaterial for Wade, who rejected all criticisms as without scientific basis, made by people who had not actually read his book (Evans 2018). According to the anthropologist Alex Golub, this was baseless because the letter's signatories were not even the 'die-hard anti-Wade contingent' and the book had been discussed at length in genetics circles before the letter had even been written (Golub 2014). While some involved in these debates may wish for the matter to remain confined to academia, the politics of genetics and IQ cannot be ignored, particularly as they run rampant through the microcosms of YouTube and podcasting. For example, after Donald Trump's election in 2016, Wade revisited the criticisms of his book during a conversation with the vastly popular Canadian 'race realism' propagandist Stefan Molyneux, who, at the time of writing, has 925,000 subscribers to his YouTube channel (Evans 2018). At an event in Sydney with far-right provocateur Lauren Southern, Molyneux said of white dispossession of Aboriginal land: 'They say that your ancestors tried to steal the land. I say they were trying to stop infanticide and mass rape ... I will not honour this culture' (D. Smith 2018).

In our times, a central conduit for ideas such as those promulgated by non-scientists – who nonetheless claim the language of science – about the links between race, intelligence, poverty, criminality, and educational attainment is the rise of far-right YouTubers and podcasters such as Molyneux or the 'radical atheist' and Islamophobe Sam Harris. As Flavia Dzodan notes, in our digital era, a direct link is being established between gut feeling and policy. She cites the CEO of one marketing firm who describes how a new practice known as 'opinion mining' 'uses the latest advances in artificial intelligence (AI) to mine public opinion for sentiment' (Dzodan 2017). The collection of the data on social media users' collective feelings can be used to better sell them products, as those on Facebook well know. However, similar data – X% of people agree with a statement such as 'Muslims are dangerous', 'Black people abuse welfare because they are lazy' – are used to fuel the campaigns of 'charismatic bigots' (Dzodan 2017). In parallel, 'race realism' takes hold because many white people in societies of the Global North, in the face of what they perceive as the hegemonic dictum that racism is a moral wrong, look for evidence to undergird their feeling that their culture has been supplanted by undeserving immigrants (Caldwell 2009), or that Black and Indigenous people have been the beneficiaries of unjustified attention or assistance. Given the role played by what Dzodan calls this 'collective affect', it is necessary to ask serious questions about whether established antiracist discourse can dislodge pop race science and demography.

Race: the social construction of what?

The work, most prominently, of anthropologist Franz Boas and sociologist W. E. B. Du Bois in the early twentieth century went a long way to establishing the predominantly correct view that race has no basis in actual physical differences between groups of human beings.[5] The anthropologist of race Ashley Montagu, concerned about the Nazis' eugenicist practices, agreed (Montagu 1962). Following the end of Nazi rule, the idea that race is socially constructed became widely – if not universally – accepted in scientific and political circles. The most well-known exponent of the social constructionist position on race from within genetics is

Race beyond Social Construction

Richard Lewontin, who first argued in 1972 that there is more genetic difference between individuals than there is among population groups, and that 'there is no objective way to assign the various human populations to clear-cut races' (Lewontin 2006). This appeared to be borne out in broad terms by the publication of the human genome project in 2003 (El-Haj 2007).

Nevertheless, there has never been a time in which race was not in use both colloquially and by scientists. Amade M'charek reminds us that even the 1950 UNESCO 'Declaration on Race and Racial Prejudice' wished to conserve a separation between the 'fact' of biological race as it may pertain in the laboratory and the mythical nature of race as it is applied in common parlance (M'charek 2013: 431). Race is under constant, silent production, with research continuously emerging that appears to open caveats in the dominant position that there is no way to equate race with human genetic diversity (Hartigan 2008). However, the general public lack of scientific literacy, the political investment in the idea of natural racial differences that can be 'read' in our DNA, which, as I have shown, is resurgent today, as well as the popular fascination with genetics as a mode of explanation for a range of human phenomena, often leading 'to a reductive stance that biology is destiny' (Yehuda et al. 2018: 5), all conspire to make it incumbent upon us to be better at explaining *what race does*.

The explosion in popularity of DNA testing services such as 23 and Me, a company that claims to 'democratize personal genetics', is evidence of the epistemic primacy of genetics in the twenty-first century. An online search for 'DNA' will reveal a panoply of articles about whether genetics can tell your politics or whether not you are likely to be more promiscuous or monogamous. DNA ancestry testing is the object of particular popular fascination. Harvard Professor Henry Louis Gates has spurred a digital genealogy industry through his role as producer of highly successful television series such as *African American Lives*. There are a multitude of social media forums and DIY reality television-style YouTube posts in which people reveal the results of their ancestry tests. DNA testing is even proposed to have an antiracist impact, as seen in attempts to use test results to confront avowed white supremacists on the fallacy of racial purity. In one notorious case, a white supremacist activist called Craig Cobb, so convinced of his 'racial purity', took up the challenge to take a DNA test, which was revealed on American daytime talk programme *The Trisha Goddard Show*. The test revealed that 14% of Cobb's DNA came from sub-Saharan Africa, a result that he rejected as a multiculturalist plot (WYSO 2018). Indeed, research into white supremacist reactions to DNA test results revealed a tendency to 'bargain' over what percentage of white ancestry makes a person white, or to condemn ancestry testing as a whole as a 'Jewish conspiracy' if the desired results were not received (Panofsky and Donovan 2017).

DNA is the object of intense politicization, as was seen in the revelation by US Democratic senator and presidential hopeful Elizabeth Warren of the results of her DNA ancestry test in late 2018. The publication of the results was Warren's attempt to quell Republican criticisms of her claim to have Cherokee and Delaware heritage and Donald Trump's derogatory references to her as 'Pocahontas'. The test revealed that she had 'a small but detectable amount of Native American DNA' and 'concluded there is "strong evidence" she had a Native American ancestor approximately six to 10 generations ago' (McDonald 2018). However, the reliance on DNA to prove Indigenous identity directly contravenes tribal protocols for assessing membership, which do not see genetic testing as valid. As Kim TallBear remarks, 'It is one of the privileges of whiteness to define and control everyone else's identity' (Johnson 2018). TallBear contends that, rather than sitting down with tribal leaders, which the senator had repeatedly refused to do until meeting with Cherokee representatives in August 2019 during the Democratic Party primaries campaign, Warren 'privileges DNA company definitions in this debate, which are ultimately settler-colonial definitions of who is indigenous'.[6]

Assessing indigeneity according to a scale of racial purity has dangerous implications given the use of 'blood' and 'genes' to exclude rather than include. For example, Australia's far-right One Nation Party announced proposals to submit Aboriginal people to DNA testing and introduce a 'qualifying benchmark of twenty-five percent Indigenous DNA ancestry' in order to quell what it called the 'widespread "rorting" [cheating] of the welfare system'. However, there is no test for genetic Aboriginality and no Australian Aboriginal genome (Fryer 2019b). Race under settler colonialism was a project of what the late Australian historian of race and colonialism Patrick Wolfe refers to as replacement and elimination, with the ultimate aim of wresting land away from its original inhabitants for the purposes of European wealth creation. In order to achieve this, European invaders had to construct Indigenous peoples as 'maximally soluble, encouraging their disappearance into the settler mainstream' (Wolfe 2016: 39). The measurement of blood quantum was used colonially in the process of Indigenous elimination. 'Blood', as Wolfe notes, 'is like money, which also invokes liquidity to disguise the social relations that sustain it' (2016: 39). Hence to possess Aboriginal lands, white colonizers set about diluting blood, dissolving Indigenous people, and scattering those left around the landscape. The separation of Aboriginal peoples from their homelands and the forced mixing of different tribal groups on missions, under a policy euphemistically titled 'protection', was integral to the cultural genocide endured by Aboriginal peoples. This historical fact makes the appeal to racial measurement dressed up as genomic science particularly egregious to many Indigenous people within a context of ongoing colonization.

Sadly, Indigenous people's views do not stop the rise of genetic absolutism in the public sphere, with 'savvy political commentators ... taking new findings by geneticists and directly assailing social constructionist perspectives' (Hartigan 2008: 164). The problem for antiracists confronted with the resurgence of racial science among 'race realists' and their 'alt-right' mouthpieces is that the maxim that race is a social construct is often the only riposte we have recourse to. Yet, far from ending the discussion of whether biological race is real, according to anthropologist Jason Antrosio, the idea that race is a social construction is actually a 'conservative goldmine' because it was never 'connected to concrete political change' (Antrosio 2012). It is thus especially important not to leave the questioning of the social construction of race to those such as *Quillette*'s Claire Lehmann, who tweeted that 'we abhor racism yet do not believe that race is merely a social construct (another pernicious blank state dogma that has repercussions in the real world)'.[7]

Antiracists are very good at denying the biological facticity of race, but not very good at explaining *what* is social about race. Echoing Patrick Wolfe's point in this chapter's epigraph, Antrosio suggests that the social construction of race 'should have never been a stopping

point, but a way to analyse the particular circumstances that result in current configurations'. Focusing
our arguments on whether race is or is not about
biology is meaningless outside of academia because
'underlying socioeconomic structural racism is unaltered'
(Antrosio 2012). Failures to properly explicate the social
construction of race in the public domain have led to
statements such as that Eduardo Bonilla-Silva reports
hearing from a colleague: 'Race is a myth, an invention,
a socially constructed category. Therefore, we should
not make it "real" by using it in our analyses. People are
people, not black, white, or Indian. White males are just
people' (Bonilla-Silva 2018: 207). Social constructionism
lends itself to such wilfully ignorant semantic arguments.
According to Antrosio, we need to judge the theory that
race is socially constructed on whether or not it has
contributed to alleviating basic issues of racially determined power imbalances and inequality. On all measures,
Antrosio claims, it is impossible to say that it has.

This problem is not confined to the social sciences.
As John Hartigan notes, 'Genetics is not going to
provide the basis for either proving or disproving
the "social" reality of race' (Hartigan 2008: 167). If
activists and social scientists are not good at parsing
research in the natural sciences, geneticists and those in
the biomedical sciences concerned with public misinter-
pretations of their findings may not be adept at reading
the political writing on the wall which spells out that
there is no way to discuss race outside of the political
context in which it is continually reproduced. The
problem with the pure social constructionist position is
that it runs the risk of reasserting the primacy of race
as biological rather than political. In a debate with the
philosopher of race Charles W. Mills, Barnor Hesse
asks: what is race the social construction *of?* The usual

answer, he says, is 'race is a construction of the idea that there is a biological racial hierarchy'. However, this does not answer the question 'What is race?' 'In effect,' Hesse remarks 'social constructionists do not have anything to say about race that is not already said by the biological discourses' (Hesse 2013). There is abundant evidence that ideas of race developed *in situ* and that there were competing ideas among various actors within and across various colonial contexts and vis-à-vis a range of different populations about what race meant for a generalized understanding of the human (Wolfe 2016).

According to Ian Hacking in *The Social Construction of What?*, social constructionist critiques usually contain three elements: that the thing being socially constructed is neither natural nor inevitable, that it is undesirable, and that it can be changed (Hacking 2003). Hesse argues that to resolve the tautology posed by the formulation 'race is a social construction of the idea of biological race', we need an alternative account of race that goes beyond this unexplanatory circularity, because 'our account of race as a social fact cannot be the same as the very thing we're discrediting'. If race can be changed because it is not natural, we need, as Antrosio also suggests, a way of explaining how race is socially produced that proposes ways of dismantling it. And because race does not originate in nineteenth-century biological theorizations, but is, as Hesse explains, 'colonially assembled over a period of time' which goes back at least to the fifteenth century, we need more complete historical and political accounts of how race emerged and became institutionalized. What is clear is that there is no way of reducing the broad scope of racial rule to only the 'bodily or the biological' (Hesse 2013).

An associated problem is that the discussion of race has been avoided, especially in the European context. The 'silence about race' (A. Lentin 2008) masks the fact that it remains 'absently present' in domains such as 'medical practice and biomedical research, behavioural genetics and forensic policing' (M'charek et al. 2014: 462; see also El-Haj 2007). And in our networked times, a range of racial biases undergird the development of the technologies that increasingly govern our interactions with institutions and each other, such as facial recognition software that repurposes old practices of phrenology for the digital age (Breland 2017; Dzodan 2016; Gillard 2018).[8]

It is vital, therefore, to explain how the attempt to refute racial science on scientific grounds alone can be counterproductive. For example, Karen and Barbara Fields remark that, for largely cultural reasons, contemporary genetics and biomedical research often map their data onto discredited racial categories that 'make sense' for no other reason than they have made sense before. This is clear in common discourse on 'blood', as in the statement, 'even if Obama identifies as an African-American he cannot deny blood' (Fields and Fields 2012: 48). Fields and Fields remark that it should be utterly impossible to talk about blood quantum because, being a liquid, blood cannot be separated into parts. However, this does not change the fact that not only do people indeed talk about bloods as separable, but the quantification of different blood 'parts' was the basis for laws governing Indigenous populations in colonized countries, such as Australia and the US. It was also integral to the US Jim Crow-era 'one-drop rule', according to which any level of African ancestry made a person Black and necessitated segregation, as well as to the Nazi regime's assessment of the degree of

Jewishness on the basis of heredity. Nevertheless, there is a problem in dismissing race as entirely fictitious if doing so leads to denying the fact that race – not as science but as rule – continues to govern the socio-economic positioning and 'vulnerability to premature death' of variously racialized groups in society to the benefit of white people (Gilmore 2006: 28). We cannot disentangle the fact that a taxonomy of biological race is invented from the equally true fact that the experience of being ruled by racial technologies of power from birth can have a physical impact on the individual's racialized body as well as a psychological effect on the mind (Kellermann 2013; Schuller 2017; Wynter 1999).

As Amade M'charek explains, race is both fact and fiction. The facticity of race relies on the fictional narratives that are woven around it to fix it in place. Using examples that demonstrate how the idea of biological race is situated in relational practices, she shows how race is not in, but rather *of*, the body. Race cannot be isolated as any one biological or genetic fact. To produce race as a cause for a particular phenomenon, for example a crime, an illness, or a behavioural disposition, requires it to be produced in relation to a host of other signifiers. In one case M'charek describes, CCTV footage of two people accused of stabbing a young man in Brussels in 2006 was used to infer their identity as Moroccan. Although the footage provided no clear evidence of the perpetrators' ethnicity, emphasis was placed not only on phenotypical markers, such as skin colour, but also on a range of other extrinsic factors, such as clothing said to be typically worn by young North African men. Eventually, when one of the attackers was identified by his teacher as being of Polish origin, 'the news that the suspects were not of

Moroccan descent was received as a shock in Belgium' (M'charek 2013). M'charek shows how, just as racial facts are attached to fictions in order to create the necessary narrative that makes race the determining factor in a given scenario, these fictions can also come unstuck. This can be seen in assumptions that when a violent attack is carried out by a Black or Brown person, it is that person's racialized status that is to blame. Individual cases are then used to prove the general prevalence of violence among all members of the group, the most obvious case in point being Muslim people and terrorism. Race, in this scenario, magically disappears when the perpetrator is white and emphasis is placed on his (it is most commonly a man) status as a 'lone wolf', motivated by mental health problems (Bayoumi 2017) or, even more worryingly in terms of its rising acceptability, 'legitimate' concerns about immigration. For example, following the murder of Muslims in Christchurch in March 2019, the editor of *The American Conservative*, Rod Dreher, wrote that Brenton Tarrant's manifesto was 'grounded in both paranoid, racist grievance, and legitimate, realistic concerns' about 'declining numbers of ethnic Europeans' (Singhal 2019).

Beyond culture versus biology

In 2009, the *American Journal of Physical Anthropology* published a symposium titled 'Race Reconciled' in which the authors revisited arguments about the biological facticity of race in order to flesh out whether or not social constructionism was a useful explanatory approach (Antrosio 2011). Medical anthropologist Clarence Gravlee's contribution raises interesting questions for the relationship between race and biology in ways that support the social constructionist view without ignoring the bodily effects of race (Gravlee 2009). Gravlee argues that discussions about the persistence of race in the US turn on the question 'Does race exist?', leading to fruitless debates about whether race has a basis in biology. In actual fact, we should be asking 'in what ways race exists as a sociocultural phenomenon that has force in people's lives – one with biological consequences' (Gravlee 2009: 47). Race is *not* biology, he argues, but it may *become* biology.

According to Gravlee, discussions about whether race is biological or cultural operate with a confusion between genetics and biology. This can be observed in the biomedical research literature in the US, which often claims equivalence between the prevalence of certain diseases among particular racial groups and their presumed underlying genetic make-up. For example, a 2007 study of racial inequalities in pre-term birth was widely reported to provide evidence for 'important genetic contributors to the timing of birth' (Kistka et al. 2007). However, the study did not actually present any genetic data. The authors merely inferred a genetic cause from the residual differences found between Black and white mothers. As Gravlee notes, 'This finding does not warrant the conclusion that racial inequalities are genetic in origin; genetic hypotheses require genetic data' (Gravlee 2009: 49).

In the face of the popular representation of this type of research and the very real policy implications it can have, we are faced with significant challenges if we want to refute the conflation of genetics with biological race and give meaning to the statement that race is a social construct. Current evidence from population genetics demonstrates that there are more similarities than differences between groups traditionally defined as races, and that existing genetic variation does not map neatly onto these racial groups. However, it still contends that there is *some* degree of genetic variation between groups in the population that have been labelled as 'races'. This opens the door to those who want to retain race as a way of thinking about human genetic variation and is fodder for the 'race realists', what Antrosio calls a 'conservative goldmine'. Gravlee claims that saying that it is possible to identify clusters within the human population that can be mapped onto 'races' does not mean that these clusters are naturally occurring, as racial theory implies (Gravlee 2009). More or fewer clusters have been identified by different researchers over time, thus proving that there is nothing inevitable about identifying these formations. However, proponents of the social construction of race position cannot stop at the claim that there is not *enough* genetic variation between groups traditionally thought of as races to prove that they exist. Lewontin's 'argument that conventional racial classification accounts for only 5–10% of human genetic variation' allows those who believe in race to say that there is at least some consistency between human population genetic variation and race, which is enough to maintain the idea of race (Lewontin 2006). This point recalls Dzodan's important note about the role of 'gut feeling' in conjuring up racial certainties.

One reason why some researchers continue to use race as a way of distinguishing between groups in the population is its utility to the biomedical profession, which is able to map complex genetics data onto common-sense ideas about racial divisions in ways that ring true to the public, to policy-makers, and to pharmaceutical companies. As Fields and Fields discuss, for example, sickle cell anaemia is still considered a 'black disease', despite overwhelming evidence to the contrary, because the power of what they call 'folk precepts' makes the 'racial' and the 'genetic' analogous (Fields and Fields 2012). Sickle cell disease is defined in the 1972 Sickle Cell Control Act brought into effect in the US under Richard Nixon as 'an inherited blood disorder'. Because of the popular confusion between race, genetics, and blood, this entered into public consciousness through tacit endorsement by scientists despite the fact that sickle cell anaemia also affects groups who are not Black, often leading to their misdiagnosis. The US and other colonial countries have a long history of experimentation on racially marginalized populations. The infamous Tuskegee syphilis experiment, for example, tested the 'belief that syphilis killed black and white patients differently though the test involved black subjects only' (Fields and Fields 2012: 53). The experiment, run by the US Health Service between 1932 and 1972, allowed researchers to study the disease's natural course over time. It involved making Black syphilis sufferers believe they were being given a cure for the disease while actually being denied the necessary penicillin, leading to their eventual deaths.

Cardiovascular disease (CVD) is a particular lightning rod for race, as well as the class and gender assumptions with which they intersect. Janet Shim's research into the politics of CVD epidemiology notes the biopolitical nature of this field of research, involved as it is in 'tying together statistics about individuals and populations with particular conceptions of the "problem" of health, disease, morbidity and mortality' (Shim 2014: 50–1). A central concern for epidemiologists is risk prevention, and, to this end, statistics are deployed to calculate the probability of particular diseases among sectors of the population which are rendered in terms of race, class, and ethnicity. As a discipline, epidemiology requires the identification of previously unexplored risk factors to maintain legitimacy. In this context and 'under the intense surveillance of epidemiologic cohort studies, individuals classified as distinct groups and populations characterized by particular risk factors become sites for the further production of epidemiologic knowledge on cardiovascular risk' (Shim 2014: 60). For Shim, then, 'culture' becomes a 'proxy for pathology in CVD research and treatment', and recognizing risk variations among groups in the population leads to 'working-class people of colour' in particular being treated as culturally inferior (Grzanka et al. 2016: 28).

Relatedly, the heart failure drug BiDil is specifically marketed to Black patients in the US. Most drugs developed in the US are tested on white people yet marketed to the population as a whole. However, in the case of BiDil, only Black patients were studied and a specific drug was developed for Black heart disease sufferers. BiDil is sold at seven times the cost of similar drugs used for non-Black patients. It can thus be highly profitable to suggest that groups designated as races suffer from particular diseases or suffer from them in particular ways based on a problematic connection drawn between race and genetics, and an even more problematic assumption that different 'races' have different kinds of blood, as in the case of sickle cell anaemia. Patrick Grzanska and his co-authors argue that bioethicists must take an intersectional approach that would zoom in on how the interplay between interlocking systems of 'racism, sexism, heterosexism and ableism' produces inequality in the research and treatment of disease (Grzanska et al. 2016: 27). But it is debatable what impact this would have in a world in which race has been commodified in biomedicine, as the BiDil example shows. Nadia Abu El-Haj signals the role that individuals play in this too, not just as patients but as 'consumers in waiting' (El-Haj 2007: 293). As in the case of DNA testing, the certainties that race seems to provide, and which individuals crave, mean that the public also participates in the move to see the world in genomic terms. The state, on the one hand, imposes an order on an uncertain world by, for example, approving drugs such as BiDil, which 'implies recognizing the biological reality of race'). But, on the other hand, it does so in response to the demands both of the profit-driven biomedical industry and of consumers sold a new horizon of 'personalized medicine' (El-Haj 2007: 293).

Refuting the existence of race, however, is not the same as saying that there is no such thing as human biodiversity and that groups who are racialized differently may require different forms of treatment for physical and mental illness. According to Gravlee, diversity, whether cultural or genetic (and these registers are often conflated), is not the problem; the problem is the persistence of white supremacy based on the belief that diversity is hierarchical (Gravlee 2009). We cannot discuss diversity neutrally because it is imbued with racial meaning. Different groups in the population who have traditionally been thought of as races may indeed suffer differently and have a higher incidence of certain diseases. A good example in Australia is the higher prevalence of diabetes among certain Aboriginal people.[9] This cannot be explained without shedding light on how techniques of race produce these bodily inequities, including through the denial of Aboriginal people's connection to their traditional food sources owing to their removal from ancestral lands (Foley 2005) and the contemporary unaffordability of fresh produce in many Aboriginal communities (Stoneham 2017). We must explain these differences without succumbing to simplistic biological accounts that suggest that there is a natural predisposition of Aboriginal people to diabetes, rather than a colonially produced effect on health. The very real fact that racial rule produces inequities between groups construed as separate races means that people, such as Aboriginals in Australia or Black people in the US, among whom there is more socioeconomic deprivation over generations get more sick. Racial rule, thus, has a biological effect both on the individual body and on bodies over generations. It is not that Black or Aboriginal people start off with a genetic predisposition to contracting particular diseases, but that the effects of colonization, slavery, and the resultant inequality and discrimination can begin to make generation after generation sick.

Epigenetic potential?

The potential of epigenetics for theorizing how 'heredity material is shaped by life events' is an area of research gaining more attention (Schuller 2017: 210). Studies of the intergenerational effects of trauma propose that people can inherit the effects of their progenitors' experiences. In the most widely discussed research on descendants of Holocaust survivors, geneticists proposed that 'effects of a parental trauma could persist into the next generation though epigenetic marks encoded on DNA and passed through the germ line' (Yehuda et al. 2018: 2). This does not cause mutation of the gene itself but rather alters the way in which the gene is expressed by damaging its functioning proteins (Carey 2018). For Kyla Schuller, these new findings in epigenetics map onto a nineteenth-century history of the role of what she calls 'sentimental biopolitics' in the development of 'modern concepts of race, sex and species' (Schuller 2017: 5). Her discussion foregrounds one of the major difficulties in developing understandings of race that grasp at its complexity while being accessible to the public.

The idea that race is a social construction of the idea of biological race relies on the notions, first, that there was agreement on what precisely biological races looked like, and, second, that these were arranged according to a hierarchy of immutable categories. In fact, Schuller argues, race and sex were never static or insurmountable in nineteenth-century accounts. Plasticity was emphasized over determinism. The major distinguishing factor between 'civilized' and 'primitive' bodies was gauged by their assumed capacity for 'impressibility', the degree to which the nervous system can be altered by external agents 'over evolutionary time' (Schuller 2017: 7). Those possessing 'civilized bodies' were theorized as being able to modulate how susceptible their senses were to the world around them and, as a population, develop stronger resistance to it. In contrast, 'primitive bodies' were 'deemed to be impulsive and insensate, incapable of evolutionary change, whose existence was very close to running out of time' (Schuller 2017: 4). Settlers on stolen Aboriginal lands, for example, were said to be adaptable to a society under construction, in contrast to 'natives', who were assimilated only with nature and thus incapable of accommodating to new realities, an idea that could not be further from the truth given the capacity of Aboriginal people for survival (Wolfe 2016). Schuller's account sheds light on how race works analogously to a valve which opens and closes to diversely include and exclude so that groups are racialized differently over time and space and in relation to the political demands of the day. The regulation of feeling that she describes also signals that race is best thought about alongside accounts of how the constraining structures of nation, gender, heterosexuality, and class are set up to create order amid the messy realities of actually existing human life.

For Schuller, Wolfe, Antrosio, Hesse, and Gravlee, social constructionism has reached the end of its utility. Schuller remarks that the social constructionist position on race sees the material body as a 'passive receptor of social scripts' (Schuller 2017: 206). She argues that the social constructionist idea that the body responds to culturally produced stimuli, but not vice versa, deepens rather than disrupts the power of race and sex as technologies of power. Culture or socialization are easily interchangeable with race as a naturalized rationale for inequality (Lentin 2014a). Social constructionism sought to put the lie to the idea that bodies could be perfected through eugenicist practices in order to yield the 'racially superior' and breed out the 'feeble races'. The focus on the abhorrence of these ideas and the decision that they were motivated by an ideology of racism, as we shall see in the next chapter, further obscured the extent to which they remain fundamental to the race project under different guises. As Cheryl Harris shows in her study of how whiteness was made property in the US – a settler colonial society founded on dispossession and slavery – the entire object of race as heredity is to render whiteness both superior and inherently precarious, thus necessitating protection (Harris 1993; see also Schuller 2017). We can understand the resurgence of biological race, seeping from the political fringes into the mainstream under the guise of 'race realism', as connected to the continued need to rescue whiteness from perceived demographic overrun by 'primitive' bodies (asylum seekers, Palestinians, Muslims, etc.). 'White genocide' is nothing short of a

The entire object of race as heredity is to render whiteness both superior and inherently precarious, thus necessitating protection.

breath-taking, albeit knowing, subversion of the actual histories of genocide against Indigenous peoples around the world, and against Jews and Roma people.

It is also no accident that racial determinism appears to be gaining in public acceptability when the final nail in the coffin of multiculturalism has been well and truly hammered in (Lentin and Titley 2011). 'Race realists' propose that 'dangerous left-wing' beliefs in human hybridity which provided the ideological framework for 'mass migration' into the imagined homogeneous cultural spaces of the West are responsible for societal disarray. The division of the world's populations along traditional racial lines, each with its own 'natural' corresponding geographical space, has thus been shattered. Put this way, the political implications of 'race realism' become clear: while western governments of all political stripes may not refer openly to the language of biological race, they all advocate for the control of migration along racial lines and enact discriminatory policies which reproduce race internally. They may not endorse the language of 'white genocide', but their practices suggest the tacit acceptance of what that implies. How else might we explain the passage by the social democratic Danish government of over 100 new laws regulating migration and the lives of migrants, asylum seekers, and their descendants, including a burqa ban and the designation of twenty-nine areas as 'ghettos'? (Macdonald 2019). Such policies conceive certain bodies as being 'out of place'. We cannot then discuss them without thinking about how the body is the primary carrier of race and how bodies are collectively turned into populations to be regulated and confined. In other words, we cannot overlook the body as a racial frontier. Knowing that this is socially constructed does not overcome the effects of the ways in which race is lived in the body, both by those racialized as other than white, and by those for whom maintaining racial boundaries around what they have amassed – as individuals, as institutions, or as geopolitical entities – is vital for survival.

Schuller suggests that, while epigenetics research does not overturn dominant accounts of sex and race as immutable, it nonetheless has the capacity for seeing 'the body as an assemblage of corporeal and environmental processes' (Schuller 2017: 210). Might epigenetics provide the key for how the experience of being racialized or gendered takes hold in the body rather than being just an idea? Alexander Weheliye's focus (Weheliye 2014), following Hortense Spillers (Spillers 1987), on how racializing assemblages make the suffering body into flesh also gestures towards the problematic divide between the bodily and the sociopolitical in most accounts of race. Far from using the findings from epigenetics research to see heredity as destiny, as is the case in most interpretations (Yehuda et al. 2018), Schuller suggests we follow Silvia Wynter (Wynter 1999), who emphasizes what the radical anticolonial psychiatrist and theorist of the Black condition Frantz Fanon called 'sociogeny' (Fanon 1986 [1967]), the binding together of nature and culture in determining individual experience. Seeing the relationship between the body and the social world in this way could go some way towards showing how psychology and physiology are also important in assessing the individual effects of material racialized and gendered inequities.

Yet current interest in the epigenetic transmission of trauma signifies the dangers, already alluded to, of conducting discussions of the biological effects of race, culture, and inheritance in an apolitical register. There is always the potential for the findings of epigenetics research and the idea of biological plasticity to be used to propose eugenics-type policies. Schuller suggests that giving expression to how race resides in the body not only as inherited trauma but as also as identity has the capacity to generate new forms of resistance against the inevitabilities that racialization reproduces, even if that identity is derived from being racialized against one's will . This is supported by Rachel Yehuda and her co-authors' study of inherited Holocaust trauma, which insists that, far from the traumatic effect on individuals being permanent, it is 'as likely to foster resilience as vulnerability' (Yehuda et al. 2018: 5).

The conditions of invention

This chapter has shown how repeating the mantra that race is a social construction is not enough to dismantle its effects on either the social or the physical body. Mainstream antiracism that relies predominantly on this stance is ill equipped to counter the ahistorical redefinition of racism as a universal form of prejudice. The critique of antiracism from both the right and the left of politics cannot be withstood if we do not engage in a much more historically situated account of how race is produced and reproduced on a range of registers: economic, political, corporeal, and environmental. The fundamental truth about race, that it is in constant need of replication owing to its inherent instability, is illustrated by Patrick Wolfe. Wolfe contrasts the meanings of blackness and indigeneity under racial colonialism (Wolfe 2016). During the US regime of slavery, blackness signified the inherited status of enslavement. The maternal body was the literal site where race was reproduced, as someone born to an enslaved woman automatically became enslaved themselves. Unlike in the case of the Indigenous peoples who had to be ushered out to clear the land, the Black body had to be continually reproduced to ensure a constant, inter-generational labour supply (Harris 1993). In contrast, following the incipient attempts at total genocide, the colonial management of Indigenous populations in North America and Australia proceeded by attempting to 'breed nativeness out' through what Wolfe calls a 'biogenetic expansion of frontier homicide' (Wolfe 2016: 11).

The fact, evidenced by the 'one-drop rule', that acceding to whiteness is seen as impossible for the Black population while desirable for the Indigenous population, and that both these views serve to solidify white dominance, reveals the ultimate unsteadiness of race and why it requires constant remaking (Wolfe 2016). Nevertheless, this inherent instability, while pointing to the myriad ways in which race can be challenged and critiqued, does not mean that we are about to witness the collapse of racial rule. Necessity – in this case the necessity of maintaining the global colonial order to which ideas of racialized advantage are fundamental – is the mother of (re)invention.

Race, thus, predates the era with which it is most often associated, the so-called nineteenth-century 'golden age' which saw the rise to dominance of biological deter-minism in all areas: reproductive, familial, political, economic, and social, in addition to the scientific. More than an idea, as I proposed in the Introduction, it is a practice; a mechanism for sifting and classifying the world, declaring parts of it *Terra Nullius* and placing the populations living there outside the realms of humanity to achieve colonial domination. Nonetheless, much of the debate about whether race is real or socially constructed does not take into account the fact that race predated its theorization as biology, developing in stages and relying on a range of accounts including the religious and the cultural after 1492 (S. Hall 2017). Discussions focus on whether or not race exists rather than on *the capacity for racial logics to adapt* (Chun 2012; Muñoz 2006). The very discussion about whether or not race is really descriptive of differences between human groups exists because of the power that race has had to arrange and structure our understanding of the relationship between the different parts of the world and its people since the invasion of the Americas, thus creating a vicious circle from which it is difficult to escape.

In the next chapter, I argue that the debate about the uses of race is further muddied by the suggestion that it is motivated only by an ideological commitment to racism. This view of race as narrowly commensurable with its theorization as science does not take into account the longer *durée* of the racial-colonial and lends itself to facile adjudications of what is and is not racism, a question wholly bound up with the acceptability of contrarian 'race realism' in the public sphere at a time of mounting white supremacism. This is not a purely academic conversation, but academics do play a central role in it. Indeed, those most visibly claiming to bravely speak uncomfortable truths about race, migration, and Islam against what they misrepresent as the antiracist orthodoxy are academics, many of whom have highly rewarded positions at some of the world's most prestigious institutions. Their claim of marginalization is thus disingenuous, but effective, and serves to present repackaged eugenicist ideas as legitimate scholarly offerings on a so-called 'marketplace of ideas', that most apt of adaptations of the fiction of the free market as a neutral arbiter.

This could be seen in the case of Cambridge University's decision to withdraw the fellowship of 'race realist' social scientist Noah Carl in May 2019, which prompted prominent figures among a cohort of highly mediatized academics to rush to his defence. Despite Carl having contributed to the conference on eugenics secretly held annually at University College London between 2014 and 2018 and the replication of his research on racial stereotypes by far-right websites (van der Merwe 2018) the Birkbeck College political scientist Eric Kaufmann concluded that Carl's dismissal was 'a victory for the Leftist-Modernist Inquisition based on guilt-by-association and abandoning the defense of free enquiry'.[10] *Quillette* magazine's characterization of Carl's scholarship as 'defending intelligence researchers who've written about the taboo topics of race, genes and IQ and argu[ing] that stifling debate in these areas is likely to cause more harm than allowing them to be freely discussed by academics' is key to understanding how, in the face of hegemonically produced racial illiteracy, a contrarian elite peddling its own fictitious victimization is strongly positioned to establish the grounds for how racism is defined (*Quillette* 2018). Who may and may not define racism, and how this relates to race as rule, is the subject to which I now turn.

2

'Not Racism™'

At this point those who use the terms 'racially tinged' or 'racially charged' to describe white supremacy should be prepared to explain why they chose to employ those terms instead of 'racist'/'racism.' If the answer is their own discomfort, they're protecting the wrong people.
Tweet by US Congresswoman Alexandria Ocasio-Cortez, 12 January 2019 (Rojas Weiss 2019)

In late 2018, the euphemization of racism went viral. It seemed that suddenly Internet users were waking up to the ridiculous contortions that the media were getting into to avoid describing a person or a situation as racist. In the US, against the backdrop of increasingly brazen support for white supremacism, facilitated though not instigated by the Trump presidency, activists and writers were pointing out the media's discomfort with naming racism. In one striking example, a single *Washington Post* article spoke of 'racial insults', 'racial undercurrents', 'racial animosity', 'racial fringes', 'racial attacks', 'racial connotations', and 'racial fears' to describe the so-called 'stoking [of] racial animosity' by Republicans (Glickman 2018). In January 2019, new US Congress member Alexandria Ocasio-Cortez addressed the issue head-on, challenging the media for their failure to name Iowa representative Steve King's open support for white supremacist positions and white nationalist organizations as racist (Zatat 2019). Journalist Yashar Ali reported that NBC News had sent guidance to its journalists 'that they shouldn't refer to Steve King's comments as racist. Instead they said reporters should say, "what many are calling racist," or something like that.'[1]

On the other side of the globe, that January, like every January since 1788, was a traumatic month for Aboriginal people in Australia. It is not that the month brings more structural injustice than any other in a country where Aboriginal life expectancy is ten years lower than the average (AIHW n.d.) and where every child in juvenile detention in the Northern Territory is Aboriginal (Allam 2018). It is that the opportunity to debate the legitimacy of celebrating the nation on the day of colonial invasion rubs salt into these still-open wounds. In January alone, five Aboriginal girls under fifteen took their own lives (Fryer 2019a). This did not deter the repetition of well-worn racist tropes by morning-show host Kerri-Anne Kennerley, who questioned whether any of those marching in Invasion Day protests had 'been out to the outback where children, babies, five-year-olds are being raped, their mothers are being raped, their sisters are being raped' (Dodson 2019).

Kennerley claimed offence after her remarks were called racist by fellow panellist Yumi Stynes. Aboriginal writers, commentators, activists, and social media users spent the last days of a January already infused with deep exhaustion responding to the inevitable outpouring of racist denial that followed the incident. Fiona Nicoll's observation that 'the very idea of suggesting that someone might be racist has been elevated into a crime to rival (if not displace) racism itself' was echoed in these responses (Nicoll 2004). For Aboriginal leader Shannan Dodson, Kennerly's behaviour was a 'common example of how deeply offended people become when they are called out for racist behaviour, which is touted as much more offensive than actually being racist' (Dodson 2019). Indeed, the Australian Communications and Media Authority was to take Kennerley's side in the dispute, finding that her remarks did not breach its code and thus had not provoked 'intense dislike, serious contempt or severe ridicule against a person or group of people because of age, colour, gender, national or ethnic origin, disability, race, religion or sexual preference' (Kelly 2019).

Racism is denied and offence is taken because naming racism is heard as an outrageous accusation (Ahmed 2016). No one is a racist. As Eduardo Bonilla-Silva tells it in his classic text *Racism without Racists*, all whites but the members of white supremacist organizations mobilize 'sincere fictions' to claim they are not racist (Bonilla-Silva 2018: 1). Beyond the 'colourblind America' of Bonilla-Silva's description, there are no racists either. From this perspective, Australian senator and former major-general Jim Molan is not a racist, despite the fact that in 2018 he shared fake Islamophobic videos put out by the far-right Britain First party on Facebook. Molan was one of the architects of Australia's punitive asylum seeker policy 'Operation Sovereign Borders', which since 2013 has required any asylum seeker who attempts to arrive to Australia by boat to be detained on one of two Pacific islands, Manus in Papua New Guinea and Nauru in Micronesia. He has also been accused of war crimes for his role as commander of US coalition forces in Iraq (Wareham 2018). Addressing the accusations that his Islamophobic statements on social media were racist, Molan said, 'I've put my life on the line for Islamic countries ... for people to say this is racist I find deeply offensive.' He claimed to have 'no regrets' for posting the Britain First videos (Lowrey 2018). In fact, Britain First itself denied its own racism, claiming on its website that 'the word "racism" was invented by a communist mass murderer, Leon Trotsky, to silence European opposition to "multi-culturalism", so we do not recognise the validity of this made-up word' (Gander 2015).

In his second line of defence, Molan argued, 'Anyone who thinks I am anti-Islamic or racist is stark raving mad – I am not either.' So, neither Australia's actions in the Iraq War nor its offshore asylum detention policy may be included in the definition of racism acceptable to him. Islamophobia, in particular, despite being a major driver of the War on Terror, is 'not racism' in Molan's view. Supporting him, the then Prime Minister Malcolm Turnbull said that Molan did not have 'a racist bone in his body' and that calling him a racist was 'disgusting' and 'deplorable' because 'he defended Australians' values in the battle against Islamist terrorism in the Middle East' (Gartrell 2018). The 'no racist bone' cliché was also the defence used by Donald Trump after he accused six Congress members, including Alexandria Ocasio-Cortez, Ayanna Pressley, Rashida Tlaib, and Ilhan Omar, all of whom are women of colour, of being 'savages'. 'Those Tweets were NOT Racist. I don't have a Racist bone in my body!' he tweeted (Bruney 2019).[2]

Beyond the role played by denial in such incidents lies racism's debatability, the 'incessant, recursive attention as to what counts as racism and who gets to define it' (Titley 2019: 8). The presentation of racism as debatable is heightened within a media landscape 'characterized by increased communicative participation through connective media, where "more talk" is a socially valorized and economically prioritized pursuit' (2019: 4). As soon as racism is mentioned, an 'invitation to refute its relevance' is proffered (2019: 2). Gavan Titley's discussion of how social media exchanges are typified by what Sanjay Sharma calls a 'racialized info-overload' illuminates the difficulty of enhancing racial literacy in public discourse (Sharma 2013). Examples from contemporary media abound, from the question posed by television documentaries with titles such as *Is Australia Racist?* (SBS 2016) to social media explorations of the true intent of Irish actor Liam Neeson's admittance that he once wanted to find any Black man to kill in revenge for the rape of a friend (Michallon 2019). Was race really at play?

The responses to Neeson shed light on how the 'not racism' I propose characterizes how we speak about racism today goes beyond denial and pseudo-humanistic declarations of colourblindness. 'Not racism' entails the constant redefinition of racism to suit white agendas, and goes to the heart of the question of who gets to define what racism is. We are long past the days of postracialism theorized by Bonilla-Silva and others. Today, defining racism has become a site of political struggle. Neeson's story is but one example, but, for Gary Younge, it had a sharpening effect:

> The next time someone asks me why I have a chip on my shoulder, I need no longer brush the question away with disdain. I can say, with all sincerity: 'Because there may well be an Oscar-nominated actor out there who wants to kill me, so I have to be alert at all times.' (Younge 2019)

The fact that Neeson asked his friend the colour of her attacker's skin can only be understood against the 'centuries-old role that black male sexuality plays in the justification of racism in general and lynching in particular' (Younge 2019). In contrast, others applauded Neeson for divulging a forty-year old story that he could easily have kept hidden as an uncomfortable but useful exercise, eliding the fact that his publicists considered that a fantasy about murdering a Black man was an acceptable narrative to draw on to promote the revenge film in which he stars, *Cold Pursuit*. One African-American conservative columnist, for example, felt Neeson uttered 'uncomfortable truths about himself and his own prejudice' as opposed to what she calls the 'extremely unhelpful ... PC script' of white guilt (K. Davis 2019). The dominant view expressed in the dismissal of Younge's fears as unhelpful political correctness is that leaping to accusations of racism is needlessly denunciatory. However, this is only possible if racism is treated as just another opinion among a 'diversity of viewpoints', which avoids the uncomfortable truth that Neeson had unconsciously or otherwise absorbed the history of white supremacism and thus 'calculated that he would be able to kill and, by deploying the legal cover of self-defence, get away with it' (Olusoga 2019).

The adjudication of whether a statement, an action, or a process is racist in our mediated public culture eschews engagement with what race *does* as a discursive and performative regime in these scenarios. The discussion of whether someone like Neeson is racist happens in unconscious comparison to hegemonic accounts of what racism is and what 'a racist' looks like. Neeson's admission is itself proffered as proof of his non-racism: 'I'm not racist,' he told *Good Morning America*. 'I'm a fairly intelligent guy and that's why it kind of shocked me when I came back to earth' (Pulver 2019). The quest for personification on both sides of the argument – those for whom Neeson has offered us a teachable moment about the universality of revenge, and those for whom he epitomizes the racism lurking behind urbane civility – bypasses a more nuanced analysis of the landscape in which these events play out. In this terrain, the question of who can control the definition of racism has grown in importance almost as a function of the lack of control that many racialized people have over the determination of their life course.

This chapter argues that the dominant conception of racism relies on a Eurocentric formulation that is unable to fully encapsulate the effects of racial rule and the logic it bequeathed on social structures and consequent individual lived experience. Racism, as I shall show, was first coined to describe a problem internal to Europe: rising antisemitism in the context of twentieth-century European fascism. At its origins, the term 'racism' did not apply to the colonial domination that existed in parallel with these intra-European political developments. And in some cases, as we shall see, a commitment to fighting racism in Europe comfortably coexisted with the belief in the racial inferiority of colonized peoples. I do not wish to discount the fact that, since first entering the lexicon in the late nineteenth century, racism has been explained and theorized in many useful ways. However, what I suggest in this chapter is that we need to interrogate its origins in order to understand what it is possible to do with the dominant explanation of racism: that it is a moral wrong based on bad science. This perspective yields a thin understanding of racism as aberrant behaviour, measurable and punishable in individuals, a view which, in turn, lends itself to becoming something that can be expressed by anyone regardless of how they are racialized.

The question of
who can control the
definition of racism has
grown in importance
almost as a function
of the lack of control
that many racialized
people have over the
determination of their
life course.

Consequently, the boundaries around what can be defined as racist extend ever outwards, especially at times of perceived crisis around racially indexed topics such as migration, crime, and terrorism (D. A. Davis 2007). This can be seen in the acceptance of terms such as 'anti-white' or 'reverse' racism, and this has serious institutional and political implications. In one case, during a discussion on a popular French TV chat show in 2007, Houria Bouteldja, the spokesperson for the decolonial antiracist group the *Mouvement des indigènes de la République*, insisted on the need to educate the white French population about the history of racism and colonialism. She used the term '*souschien*', an ironic neologism that makes reference to the category '*Français de souche*' ('of French stock'), first employed by *Front national* leader Jean-Marie Le Pen in 1979 and later taken up by French demographers to refer to 'indigenous' (white) French people, thus distinguishing from the Black and Arab population. The contrarian philosopher Alain Finkielkraut, who, as we shall see in Chapter 4, is a notorious figure in French discussions of race, chose to add a hyphen to render the word as '*sous-chien*', or 'sub-dog' (mongrel), and accused Bouteldja of anti-French or anti-white racism (Confiant 2008). Finkielkraut's provocative re-punctuation provided an example for those, among them the French republican magazine *Marianne*, keen to demonstrate how France's postcolonial citizens had been allowed too much leeway. The then French Interior Minister, Brice Hortefeux, who knew well 'that Houria Bouteldja was being ironic', was one of the first to take up Finkielkraut's call to arms. 'He declared that foreigners whom France "welcomes, hosts and feeds do not have the right to insult French people"', thus effectively denying French citizens of immigrant origin the right 'to bandy words about or make puns like any other French person' (Confiant 2008). As a direct consequence of these events, in May 2010 and again in October 2011, Bouteldja was summoned before the courts on charges of anti-French racism, the result of a case prepared against her by the *Alliance générale contre le racism et pour le respect de l'identité française et chrétienne* (AGRIF).[3] That the AGRIF emerged from agents of the fascist Vichy regime and the murderous OAS in Algeria, and had strong contemporary links to the *Front national*, illustrates the centrality of 'anti-white racism' to a right–left consensus premised on the threat posed by a rising movement of autonomous antiracist intellectuals.

In another context, the October 2019 British Equalities and Human Rights Commission (EHRC) report into racism in higher education included the category 'white British' in its survey, finding that 9% of white English students and staff experience what they called 'racial harassment'. The inclusion went against advice from academics and Black student union representatives that it was not appropriate. An EHRC representative problematically associated a 'small number of examples of anti-English sentiment at Scottish and Welsh universities' with 'offensive comments about Gypsy and Irish Traveller students and examples of anti-Semitic slurs', despite the fact that these groups occupy distinctly different racialized positions to white English people (Batty 2019).

When looked at in the context of 'not racism', what these examples show is that racism is both universalized and particularized from a structurally white perspective. On the one hand, groups who have traditionally been the objects of racial subjugation and violence are set up as today's 'real racists', while, on the other hand, when it comes to the adjudication of white racism, great care must be taken before 'jumping to conclusions'. A white understanding of white racism as excessive, aberrant, and attitudinal is useful to elites in the current political moment. The definition of 'true' racism must, it is proposed, be protected, gently wrapped in the tissue paper of 'legitimate knowledge'. This makes it near impossible to look beyond the statement 'I'm not a racist', and ask why this declaration stands in for an adequate discussion of race as a technology of power, reducing it instead to the narcissism of the question 'Are they, are we, am I racist?'

Historicizing 'not racism'

'Not racism' is a quest to control the definition of racism that enacts a discursive racist violence (A. Lentin 2018). I began tracking the narrative following the June 2017 attack on the Finsbury Park Mosque in London by Darren Osborne, who drove his van into a crowd, killing one Mosque-goer, Makram Ali, and injuring ten others. Osborne was described by his family as troubled but 'not racist'. Osborne's actions, it was claimed, were not motivated by hate. He was a 'lone wolf' who was 'complex', according to the *Telegraph* newspaper's report, despite shouting 'I'm going to kill all Muslims – I did my bit' after the attack (Ward et al. 2017). After this, I started to notice an almost daily repetition of 'not racism' declarations. 'Not racism' is packaged in a variety of ways. However, two elements always accompany the presentation of an individual or a situation as 'not racist'. First, racism is characterized as an excessive ascription. Second, alternative definitions of racism that diverge radically from what most people on the receiving end of racism understand it to be are offered in its place. The (re)definition of racism as universal, ahistorical, and a question of individual morality, rather than being structurally engendered, is the linchpin on which 'not racism' hangs.

I trace 'not racism' back to the emergence of racism as a concept, and to what we understand race to be. We have paid insufficient attention both to the conceptual development of racism and to its relationship with race, which, as I have been arguing, is a complex assemblage that is intrinsically unstable, polyvalent, and mobile (Stoler 2002: 373). If we wish to understand the longer-term intellectual context out of which the apparent contemporary primacy of 'not racism' arises, we need to look harder at the development over time of the terms we use, including those of us who consider ourselves antiracists. What Barnor Hesse has called the 'undecidability of racism', and the fact that there are competing – dominant and subordinate – understandings of what racism is, which also hang on different definitions of race, can obscure our clarity of vision (Hesse 2004). This problem does not only affect public debate, but is internal to race scholarship (Stoler 2002). However, this is not just a matter of intellectual disagreement; it is intrinsic to the unfolding of race itself, not predominantly as an ideology, but rather as a 'political technological ... organization' (Hesse 2004). In other words, what we think racism to be is shaped by and in turn impacts on what we think race is. Whether we consider race to be descriptive of some*thing*, most commonly the idea of a hierarchical taxonomy of biological population groups, or rather of a set of processes that serve to order, manage, sediment, sift, correct, and discipline, empowering some while causing others to buckle under that power, is central to how we conceive of and tackle racism.

63

'Not racism', then, goes beyond denial, both systemic and of the personal kind that accompanies 'white fragility' (DiAngelo 2018). Rather, what is generally thought of as 'real racism' is frozen in past examples that float free from the wider context within which they can be fully understood. The Nazi Holocaust, most prominently, is encapsulated by the genocide of the Jews of Europe while being severed not only from the adjacent Roma genocide but also from the racial-colonial practices which both prepared the ground for these atrocities and continued uninterrupted before, during, and after they ended (Césaire 2000 [1955]; Langbehn and Salama 2011). This paradoxically allows for racism to be (re) defined because the most commonly used examples of it – the Holocaust, Apartheid, and Jim Crow segregation (Hesse 2011) – are explained not as extreme yet consistent manifestations of racial rule, but as the expression of misguided, and even pathological, beliefs which, like these events, are also presented as being 'of the past'. Because racism is viewed as being fixed securely in history, the expression of less enlightened knowledges, any lingering racist beliefs are seen as the preserve of less progressive people. We hear this mindset in the oft-repeated liberal claims that white people are less racist than in the past, a measure gauging what people are willing to say about their beliefs rather than the extent to which race continues to structure sociality.

Racism is generally construed both as uniquely historically specific and as detachable from history, or, as I have described it elsewhere, as both frozen and motile (A. Lentin 2016). It is 'reassigned to the past through a temporal logic of white dislocation' (Yancy 2008: 236), and relocated amidst 'ungrateful' former colonial subjects, the descendants of enslaved people, and the still colonized Indigenous peoples of the settler states. As we have seen, this relocated racism is often named 'reverse' or 'anti-white' racism. It is part of the story I want to tell, but it is not the whole story. For even when racism is admitted to persist within white society, expressed by individuals or by institutions, there is a reticence to name it because of the dominance of the idea that 'real racism' is either over or extremely marginal. For many, the pastness of racism begins with the declaration of a postracial era following the election of Barack Obama to the US Presidency. However, the root of the problem is buried much deeper, arguably with the invention of racism itself.

To show how this is the case, I first analyse the birth of racism as a concept in Europe. I consider the role played by academics in sidelining structural accounts of race as it operated in colonial contexts and how it continues to pertain in the contemporary study of migration, for example. Racism is consistently presented as aberrant and pathological, rather than a reality of what Stuart Hall called 'societies structured in dominance' (S. Hall 1980). In the context of Brexit and the Trump election, anti-immigrant racism has been successfully framed as 'racial self-interest' and placed on a par with the mobilization by ethnic minority groups in self-defence. Political scientist Eric Kaufmann's proposition that the defence of white Christian identities is merely an innocuous form of identity politics provides intellectual legitimation for the discursively violent white redefinition of racism as 'not racism' (Kaufmann 2017, 2018a).

The Eurocentrism of racism

'Debatability' and 'not racism' can be seen as structured into prevailing understandings of what racism is. On the surface, this is due to the predominance of distancing and deflection as characteristic responses to accusations of racism, as demonstrated by the Kennerley and Neeson cases, and by the euphemization of racism. But these tendencies did not emerge spontaneously. Rather they can be found in the conceptualization of racism itself, which, from its inception in the late nineteenth century to its more widespread adoption in response to the growth of European fascism in the 1930s, was not attentive to the contexts of racial rule that produced racist sentiment. The failure of racial literacy is in the detachment of the structural from the attitudinal. This failure is not just one reproduced by a racially illiterate and structurally white media but is also undergirded in scholarship which contributes to the uncertainty that surrounds the question of what racism is. As we shall see, this reaches a pinnacle with the attention given to the proposal that what Eric Kaufmann calls 'racial self-interest' is 'not racism' (Kaufmann 2017). The widespread acceptance of this argument can be witnessed in the constant justifications of anti-migrant policies and public sentiment by way of the purportedly 'legitimate concerns' of white populations, or even white terrorists.

Whether race precedes racism or vice versa is a question at the heart of race scholarship. However, it is less common to ask whether racism as a concept may have its own limitations. Are dominant conceptions of racism enablers of the deliberations over what racism is or is not? The predominance of frozen accounts of racism hinge on a narrow interpretation of race as confined to nineteenth-century expressions of eugenicist racial science which led by the mid-twentieth century to their full expression in the Nazi genocide. Such a view neglects the longer *durée* of racial rule as 'colonially constituted', and its reliance on more than a biological account to theorize human difference (Hall 2017; Hesse 2016). The aim of determining the boundaries of humanity as a tool of colonial domination which necessitated the assertion of European Christian supremacy over internally and externally colonized populations was articulated well before the invention of new biological epistemologies during race's 'golden age' from the mid-nineteenth century. In fact, cultural and religious incompatibility – the predominant discourse framing opposition to migration as 'not racist' today – was integral to racial thinking from the outset. As Ann Stoler discusses, one of the main ways in which racism was expressed in colonial Indonesia was with regard to the cultural competencies that were displayed or not displayed by so-called 'natives'. Could 'natives' 'feel at home' in a European setting? ('To feel at home', she says, 'was a term used in the legal record.') Various means were put in place by Dutch colonial administrators to judge whether an individual 'native' could be said to be 'feeling at home'. More than any biological difference, the judgement of an inability to 'feel at home' was used as a means to set apart and discriminate against colonized subjects (Stoler and Lambert 2014).

To be sure, it is important to draw out the violence of racism, which is core to how Black and other racialized people understand and experience it and oppose it to an account of race which equates it with a naturalized form of identity. P. Khalil Saucier and Tryon Woods argue, for example, that the widely influential racial formation theory conceives of race both negatively, in terms of racism, and positively, in terms of racial identity (Saucier and Woods 2016; see also Omi and Winant 2013). It posits that groups were organized racially before being subjugated on the basis of race, thus minimizing the antiblack violence that they see as having brought race into being. Questions which have justly become important to the discussion of whether race preceded racism or vice versa, such as whether antiblackness is at the core of racism or whether, in contrast, it has antecedents in intra-European antisem-itism or Islamophobia, have, however, mainly elided the fact that none of these questions were of concern to early adopters of the term 'racism'. To what extent, then, does racism as it was first conceived adequately encapsulate what we are speaking about when we stress race as a form of rule which, far more than a prejudicial attitude and not exclusively a murderous ideology, underpinned colonial governance, underscoring the relationship between Europe and the rest of the globe, defining the modern era, and giving rise to persistent questions about what constitutes humanity?

Europeans who first deployed the term 'racism' in the late nineteenth century were untroubled by either antiblackness or the colonial constitution of race. Some among them were racists. Such was the case of nineteenth- and twentieth-century racial anthro-pology. Carole Reynaud-Paligot follows the trajectory of racial anthropology from the mid-1800s, from the general abandonment of anthropometry, through the excitement about new ideas of serology, and later to genetics (Reynaud-Paligot 2009). By the end of the nineteenth century, anthropology's efforts to establish standardized anthropometric classifications of racial differences were thwarted by newer research, such as that of Franz Boas, which used cranial measurements to show, contra the dominant thinking, that there was no way of delimiting racial groups, and that human mixing made it impossible to classify humans in the same way that zoologists grouped animal species (Boas

2015 [1911]). This did not deter anthropologists such as Paul Rivet or Raoul Anthony, who continued to see the value of the research and did not renounce either the conceptual utility of race or the effort to classify people.

The 1930s 'obliged anthropologists to descend from their ivory tower' (Reynaud-Paligot 2009: 30). By this time, the grand majority of anthropologists had concluded that, owing to intra-European migration, there was no way of distinguishing European races – Germans or Nordics from Slavs or Latins – and that there was no equivalence between race and nation, thus opposing racial scientists like Arthur de Gobineau and Georges Vacher de Lapouge who had cemented them together. French physical anthropologists almost unanimously denounced rising antisemitism in 1930s Europe. The French anatomist and anthropologist Paul Broca contended early on that there was no such thing as a Jewish race. Nevertheless, despite general agreement that there was 'equality among the white races' and that antisemitism was 'barbarous', the same could not be said for 'the question of equality among the races of colour' (Reynaud-Paligot 2009: 34). The focus between the two wars thus shifted to the colonial arena, which became a 'privileged terrain of anthropological observation' (2009: 15). Racial anthropology based on studies conducted on colonized peoples had a prominent place at the 1931 colonial exhibition in Paris and interest in it was 'largely shared by the colonial powers' (2009: 17).

This was the backdrop for the evolution of the concept of racism among French anthropologists. A case in point was Jacques Millot, who taught 'physiology of human races' at the University of Paris until the 1950s. Millot was an 'antiracist' activist and a member of the journal *Races et Racisme*, which was outspoken about the rise

of Nazism (Reynaud-Paligot 2009: 39. He believed
that racism was a discriminatory German ideology
separate from the practice of race science (Hund 2018).
Consistent with this was his belief, apparently gleaned
from cranial research on African-Americans, that Black
people's brains had 20% the capacity of those of whites.

A consensus on intra-European racial equality and
an objection to racist discrimination in Europe thus
coexisted with the practice of colonial racial anthropology and racial science by the same scholars. This
apparent paradox is at the root of two competing ways
of narrating racism. The first, subordinate narrative
uses a 'black analytics' to interrogate the 'colonial-racial
characterizations of the West' (Hesse 2014: 143). The
second narrative is analytically white and predominates
in the US sociology of race relations and the western
social sciences in general. It largely sees racism as an
aberration, as antithetical rather than co-constitutive of
liberalism, democracy, and the European nation-state
(Lowe 2015).

> [The] narration of racism is white analytically where it
> forecloses historical and contemporary commentary on
> the colonial-racial order of the West in analyses of modern
> social formations like capitalism, militarism, liberalism,
> democracy, nationalism, individualism and whiteness. ...
> [S]ociology's narration of racism is Black analytically
> where it interrogates these sociological foreclosures of
> colonial-racial characterizations of the West and analyses
> the routine conflation of its modern social formations
> with the normativity of white domination and non-white
> subordination. (Hesse 2014: 143)

The original European interpretation of racism saw it as
an intra-European problem born of the false distinction

made by the Germans between different groups of white Europeans (including European Jews). Those who challenged this racism, including the aforementioned anthropologists, were able to do so while tacitly condoning, or at least failing to mention, the persistence of racial-colonial domination. For Barnor Hesse, this creates both a conceptual and a constitutive 'double bind' at the heart of racism (Hesse 2004). The very racism that sidelined Black (and other racialized) thought from the academy (Morris 2017) means that we are left with a partial, white understanding of racism which presents a very different account of race, failing to think about it as 'an inherited western modern-colonial practice of violence, assemblage, superordination, exploitation and segregation' (Hesse 2016: viii).

Race and taboo

Despite the earlier practice of racial science by opponents of fascism and antisemitism such as Millot, following the Holocaust and the revelation of Nazi eugenicism, racial science became exclusively equated with Nazism. This yielded a blueprint wherein 'real' racism is not only extremist or exceptional, but also tacitly concerned with Europe's reckoning with itself. Unsurprisingly, this has impacted particularly on western European societies in which the Holocaust was enacted and with which many among its populations were complicit. Coming to terms with being the perpetrators of antisemitic genocide has, however, gone hand-in-hand with a denial of the coterminousness of the Holocaust and colonial rule and a temporal division of the European history of racism into pre- and post-Holocaust eras. After the end of the Holocaust, racism became comparable, debatable, and ultimately assessable as racism or 'not racism'. This coexisted with a strong rejection of the language of race which overlapped with the challenge to racism, as mentioned in the Introduction. Antiracialism – the objection to the use of the word 'race' – creates a taboo around race which, while in many cases is derived from a real worry that speaking about race has an unavoidable naturalizing effect, nevertheless detracts from a critique of the coexistence of official 'non-racism' and coloniality (Kerner 2007).

'Frozen' associations made between racism and the Holocaust lead to the active rejection of race as a technology of power for making sense of this. For example, contrasting British and German attitudes to the political mobilization of minority groups, Ruud Koopmans and Paul Statham remark that 'for obvious historical reasons related to the race politics of the Nazi period, race has never gained currency in postwar German political discourse' (Koopmans and Statham 1999: 677). The editors of a volume comparing immigration in New York and Amsterdam demonstrate a failure to see race as anything but a descriptor of phenotype, and therefore, in their view, irrelevant in societies which are less comfortable with using the language of race. They claim that 'in contemporary New York, "race" is basically a color word', while 'in Amsterdam, Islam (and cultural values and practices associated with it), not color-coded race, is the "bright boundary" and basis for exclusion of many immigrants and their children' (Foner et al. 2014: 137). By equating race only with skin colour, its role as a sociopolitical assemblage of power underpinning European domination both preceding and exceeding the period of Nazi rule is underplayed. Not only does this negate the significance of antiblackness in the

Netherlands, and Europe more broadly, but it also sweeps the legacy of intra-European racial rule under the rug, burying it alive (Goldberg 2009).

Beyond academia, in France particularly, conflict over the use of the term 'race' has become a considerable political fault line. As signalled by the *Marianne* headline cited in the Introduction, decolonial and political antiracists are denounced as racist for referring to race. In a November 2018 open letter signed by eighty French academics in *Le Point* magazine, decolonial scholars are condemned for an 'intellectual terrorism' that recalls Stalinism's attack on enlightened European thinkers (*Le Point* 2018). The letter was replicated in *Quillette* magazine (*Quillette* 2019). The author of one French book on the 'left and race' claims that using a 'racialist vocabulary' and distinguishing between 'white', 'Black', and 'Muslim' stands in opposition to the 'humanist and universalist ideas at the heart of the leftist struggle for the defence of human rights' (Boucher 2018). In this reading, racialized minorities reproduce racism when they support the right of Muslims to publicly practise their religion by veiling, for example, because opposition to racism should be inseparable from 'anticlericalism'. An antiracism seen as promoting the 'memories and traditions of subaltern groups' rather than advocating for 'all proletarians and "wretched of the earth"' is a dangerous US implantation (Boucher 2018).

The taboo of race relies on a singular and teleological view of race which sees it as always inevitably ending up in the attempted extermination of the Jews of Europe. This was undeniably of prime significance to the history of racism, and it is concerning that it is being forgotten and downplayed in many quarters. A 2019 study, for example, found that 'more than half of Austrians surveyed didn't know six million Jewish people were killed in the Holocaust' (Miller 2019). However, a sole focus on the racism of the Holocaust, especially one that fails to connect those events to other operations of racial rule, some of which directly impinged upon it, such as the German concentration camps in Namibia, ignores the persistence of racial rule after 1945 in colonial contexts and in the racial logics of contemporary incarceration and policing, borders and migration, social welfare, education, housing, and so on. A Eurocentric conception of racism advanced by a structurally white academy is unable to fully encapsulate colonially constituted racial domination, leaving us with a situation where, despite the competing existence of a 'black analytics', racism remains 'more objected to than understood' (Hesse 2014: 141).

The limits of comparison

The universalization of the Holocaust as the paradigm of racism posed a problem for other victims who mobilized the term to make sense of and draw attention to their own oppression. Rather than encouraging analogy and subsequent solidarity, as I further argue in Chapter 4, there has been a tendency towards comparison based on a sliding scale of racisms. As Alexander Weheliye remarks, comparison 'feeds into a discourse of putative scarcity in which already subjugated groups compete for limited resources leading to a strengthening of the very mechanisms that deem certain groups more disposable than others. In the resulting oppression Olympics, white supremacy takes home all the medals in every competition' (Weheliye

2014: 14). While certain analogies could be drawn with the treatment of the Jews – 'exclusion, discrimination, ghettoization, exterminations' – others could not, especially if they 'appeared inassimilable or incomprehensible and threatening to the privileging of the paradigmatic experience' (Hesse 2004: 14).

After the Holocaust, nonetheless, African-Americans attempted to repurpose the Eurocentric concept of racism to draw attention to the degradation of Black lives in America well after the end of slavery. The 'We Charge Genocide' petition was an attempt to force white opinion to face the convergences of the Jewish and the US Black experiences, rather than insisting on the uniqueness of the Nazi 'moment' (Hesse 2011). Stokely Carmichael and Charles Hamilton's *Black Power* introduced the concept of institutional racism as a form of internal colonialism (Carmichael and Hamilton 1969). However, both the foundational Eurocentrism of the racism concept and the continued dominance of a 'white analytics' pose a problem for the political mobilization of the term 'racism'. Polemically, Hesse suggests that neither the idea of internal colonialism nor that of institutional racism ever 'seriously challenged the post-World War II Eurocentric concept of racism' (Hesse 2011: 171).

In scholarship, the effacing of colonially constituted racial rule was replicated in the development of race relations as a field of study in US sociology from the 1930s on. This, *inter alia*, shaped how racism was understood mainly by white sociologists in the UK until the 'Empire struck back' with the explosion onto the scene in the 1980s of Black and colonial migrant scholars such as Stuart Hall, Paul Gilroy, and Hazel Carby (CCCS 2014 [1982]). US sociology focused attention away from colonialism by theorizing 'race relations' as a matter internal to the United States, and mainly focused on Black–white interactions and inequalities post-slavery. In fact, during what Zine Magubane calls the 'long era of global Jim Crow (1865–1965)', so-called 'race relations' were intimately connected to colonial projects (Magubane 2016). For example, the Chicago School sociologist Robert Park and the 'career man in Negro life' Thomas Jesse Jones (Woodson 1950: 107) were central to the attempt 'to articulate the "new South" and the "global South" as co-joined and coterminous political and economic projects' (Magubane 2016: 378). As cotton-picking in the Southern US ended after 1930, they were involved in the Togo–Tuskegee programme, in which African-Americans were trained by the Tuskegee Institute, founded by Booker T. Washington, to bring cotton-picking to West Africa in the aim of globalizing an industry built on slave labour (Zimmerman 2005).

The involvement of sociology in this colonial project illuminates the problem of compartmentalizing and euphemizing race as the study of 'race relations'. According to Magubane, race relations scholarship authorized 'a comparative sociology premised on the idea that societies are distinct, nationally bounded entities wherein social change is generated by endogenous mechanisms' (Magubane 2016: 378). It created a separation between racism – a contemporary problem internal to the US in this instance – and colonialism – which was seen as firmly in the past. Further, in both the US in general and US sociology in particular, an image of the country as *anti*-colonialist prevails. So residual racism may indeed be a relic of slavery, for example, but slavery in itself is not seen as a form of internal colonialism, not to mention the ongoing colonization of First Nations people and land. If this connection were laid bare, the US would be seen not as separate from, but as integral to the global racial-colonial project, thus clarifying the significance of transatlantic slavery for the development of modern capitalism and western enrichment (Williams and Brogan 1964).

The comparativism that drives race relations research also frames a migration studies agenda that is often hostile to using race conceptually to understand both why people migrate and the impact of racism on their lives post-migration. Many in the migration studies community, especially in Europe, tend to reject race-critical assessments of the drivers of immigration and the carceral nature of migration control. As a field, there is a tendency for migration studies to see the issue of migration as 'postracial', often cloistering it in economistic frameworks or relating it to liberal paradigms of human rights. In fact, as the militarized policing of borders and the subsequent transformation of the Mediterranean into a watery graveyard attests, race and colonially inflected environmental disaster and their by-products, war and starvation, have never been more central to migration and refugee movement (Erel et al. 2016). The elision of race as fundamental to understanding past and present migration policies has serious political consequences given the proximity of migration scholars to policy-making via the high-stakes funding awarded to research in the field as well as the proliferation of migration studies centres and consortia that work to support national and suprana-tional migration regimes (Erel et al. 2016; Grosfoguel et al. 2006; A. Lentin 2014b).

Mainstream migration studies scholars often prefer to measure racism by comparing the experiences of direct discrimination by migrants and people of colour across individual societies. For example, Adrian Favell considers that imposing a race lens on either intra-European East–West migration or Latino immigration to the US is counter-productive. For him, 'post-colonial theories of race, ethnicity and multiculturalism that clutter the shelves of bookstores and the pages of syllabi in the Anglo-American-dominated field of "ethnic and racial studies" are also ineffective and largely irrelevant in relation to these new movements in Europe' (Favell 2008: 706). However, as David Goldberg has suggested, similarly to Magubane, relational and interactive approaches to race and racism make better sense of how 'ideas and practices emanating from elsewhere are made local', because what appears 'homegrown' does not develop in isolation from the ways in which the ideas and practices of race and racism have developed in other locations (Goldberg 2015: 254). In particular, a comparative approach has tended to place historically racist states, such as South Africa and Nazi Germany, alongside each other. However, they should be more correctly seen as each having relationally influenced the other. Ignoring this and taking a comparative approach leads to the erroneous suggestion that states can be looked at in isolation as though ideas of race do not circulate globally. That they do is as true today as it was in the past, as attested to by the interminable debates about the hijab and the burqa that began with the French ban in 2004 and contaminated all western societies (A. Lentin and Titley 2011). It also implies that there are ideal-typical examples of racist states that can be compared to each other, thus excluding the much further reach of race beyond these 'frozen' prototypes and minimizing cases that are not considered as 'extreme' as the 'limited number of different models for state-based racisms' (Goldberg 2015: 252). In contrast, we can look at racisms as historically specific while still maintaining 'a focus on the (transnational) relationality of racisms across contexts' (Titley 2019: xi).

'Mission creep'

'Not racism', as we are beginning to see, builds on the Eurocentric definition of racism, its severing from a basis in colonial rule, and a strongly antiracialist drive based on the taboo of race, which replaces antiracist commitment (Goldberg 2009). It is mobilized most successfully in discussions of migration, where academics and policy-makers present immigration control as a sensible approach that has nothing to do with racism. Barack Obama, in an address to a gathering of 'young leaders' in Berlin in April 2019, proposed that 'we can't label everyone who is disturbed by migration as racist' (Da Silva 2019). Once immigration ceased to be of material necessity to European societies rebuilding after the destruction caused by the Second World War, migration controls became more a matter of culture than of economics, both of which were presented as racially neutral. In Australia, after the end of the 'White Australia Policy' in the early 1970s, albeit often exploitative labour migration could continue apace while family reunification and asylum were progressively hindered and criminalized. From the late 1970s on, after the ending of family reunification and the imposition of other restrictions on the movement of former colonial subjects to Europe, the 'real racism' of old was construed as an outdated, irrational attitude and cleansed from what became the dominant perspective on questions of migration, national identity, and citizenship. It became 'not racism' but 'commonsense'

(Bhattacharyya 2020). Today, motivated by a confected fear of dwindling white population numbers, much effort is made to assert that being anxious about the effects of migration on 'national culture' is 'not racist'. In reality, Gargi Bhattacharyya reminds us, 'controlling and shaping population movement is among the most consistently racialized practices of most contemporary states' (Bhattacharyya 2018: 129). It maps onto the longstanding racialized obsession with another aspect of population control – fecundity – and the attendant white fear that 'like weeds, these people can reproduce in the most inhospitable of circumstances' (Bhattacharyya 2018: 39).

'Not racism' also hangs on the idea that to foreground race is unscholarly. This is given weight in public discussions where currency is made by a disproportionately publicized group of academics who argue that to name racism is denunciatory rather than empirical. Most prominent among these is the aforementioned political scientist Eric Kaufmann, who asserts that white people's expression of anxiety in the face of migration may be 'racial self-interest' but it is 'not racism'.[4] He bases his theory on the myth of a hegemonic 'left-moralist' agenda which wrongly portrays the commonsense of the 'ethnic majority' as racist (Kaufmann 2018a). Antiracists are caricaturized as an anti-free speech 'mob', while his own analysis, grounded in attitudinal surveys and social psychological theorizations, is presented as sober and detached. A large part of the success of 'not racism' is its proponents' ability to portray themselves as the defenders of Enlightenment rationality and free inquiry against an authoritarian antiracist hegemony that finds academic legitimacy in what they propose is the unscientific domain of critical race theory. While Kaufmann and his associates, such as the theorist of national populism Matthew Goodwin, pin their colours to the mast by defending discredited racial science contrarian Noah Carl, the questioning of the legitimacy of critical race scholarship is also a mainstay of less contentious areas of academia (Kaufmann 2019). As we have seen, migration studies scholar Adrian Favell rejects critical race theory as an imprecise mode of analysis and lauds research that moves beyond what he calls 'purely denunciatory work on the negative consequences of immigration (such as studies of racism)' (Favell 2003: 20). How does the idea that racism is used too imprecisely move out of academia to inform and shape public discussions, and what is the role of the media-friendly academic in whitewashing 'not racism'?

If critical race studies emphasize the structural, 'not racism' is a sentiment dressed up as serious science, recalling once again Flavia Dzodan's reflection on the political salience of 'gut feeling' (Dzodan 2017). Eric Kaufmann's 2017 study of Leave and Remain voters in the UK Brexit referendum and Trump and Clinton voters in the US 2016 presidential elections was presented in a report by the UK think-tank Policy Exchange entitled 'Racial Self-Interest is Not Racism', and later in a full-length, much-publicized and -reviewed book, *Whiteshift* (Kaufmann 2017, 2018a). Kaufmann proposes that white Christian 'ethnotraditonalism' is one among an array of available identifications, and that seeking to defend it against non-European immigrants is mere racial self-interest and 'not racism'. Kaufmann cites the longtime opponent of what he sees as the UK's overly open attitude to migration and multiculturalism, writer and quangoist David Goodhart, who claims that racism 'has been subject to mission creep'. Goodhart proposes that applying the label of racism to concerns about immigration leads to 'those in public debate [being unable to] draw a distinction between group partiality and a racism based on the fear, hatred or disparagement of outgroups' (Kaufmann 2017: 2).[5] 'Racial self-interest' cannot be equated with 'real' racism. 'The challenge here', Goodhart proposes, 'is to distinguish between white racism and white identity politics. The latter may be clannish and insular, but it is not the same as irrational hatred, fear or contempt for another group – the normal definition of racism' (Goodhart 2017b). This view is one logical outcome of the dominant idea that racism is an aberrant attitude.

The idea of a 'normal definition' of racism performs the separation between rationality and irrationality and is itself central to a racial epistemology. In fact, it is untrue to say that racism is always irrational on either logical or moral grounds. To determine the morality of racism, 'we cannot, on pain of circularity, simply claim its immorality a priori and infer its irrationality from this' (Goldberg 1990: 337). In fact, it is easier to find historical examples of people enacting racism 'rationally' given the benefits that racial discrimination has had, and continues to have, for the racially dominant, both personally and in terms of whole societies. Slavery is the prime example of this (Harris 1993). We only need to consider that former slave owners were paid compensation for the loss of 'their slaves' after the official abolition of slavery to see how this is the case. As research by the historian Catherine Hall has shown, many among Britain's elites continue to benefit financially from this compensation, including former Prime Minister David Cameron (C. Hall 2013).

Goodhart, Kaufmann, and other proponents of 'not racism' bracket the workings of racial capitalism off from their identification of 'the normal definition of racism', which is confined to the irrational attitudes of outlier groups. Such a view is derived from a social psychological approach to racism which dominates the field, particularly in the US, conflicting with the view Kaufmann presents of critical race studies as hegemonic. The failure to ground social psychological research in a critical history of racial formation leads to 'racial self-interest' being theorized as a question of 'in-group favoritism and out-group animosity', as the author of another book on 'White Identity Politics' puts it (Illing 2019; see also Jardina 2019). Structural accounts are disregarded in favour of individual ones, with Kaufmann even going so far as to argue that the now banned policy of 'red-lining' in US real estate, which effectively led to the segregation of urban neigbour-hoods on Black–white lines, was not about racism but about 'individual choices about where to live' (Chotiner 2019). Kaufmann's resistance to accounts of racism as structural rather than purely attitudinal relies on an unempirical assertion of racism as a question of diverse 'psychological profiles'. Some people, he suggests, are suited to 'cosmopolitanism' and others to 'ethnotra-ditional nationalism'. He argues that 'imposing either on the entire population is a recipe for discontent because value orientations stem from heredity and early life experiences' (Kaufmann 2018a: 12). However, because he denies the validity of structural accounts of race, Kaufmann is unable to explain the origins of these beliefs. His may be an extreme example of the separation between structure and the individual, but it is one that is generated by the dominant notion that race equates to identity and racism to attitude. Even when structural, or in this case institutional, racism was recognized by the Macpherson inquiry into the London Metropolitan police's mishandling of the inves-tigation into the 1993 murder of Black teenager Stephen

Lawrence, it was recognized 'in such a way that racism is *not seen* as an ongoing series of actions that shape institutions' (Ahmed 2004, emphasis in original).

Kaufmann's reliance on attitude surveys to assess racism, which is narrowly defined as irrational, exclusionary, and hierarchical, allows him to separate between racist and non-racist sentiments in order to build what he suggests is a more complex picture of the nuances of 'racial self-interest'. His universalist interpretation of racism severs it from what Miri Song calls its 'historical basis, severity and power' (Song 2014: 125; see also Saucier and Woods 2016). This psychologizing of race, re-expressed as inherent tribalism, has a particular lineage, one that in Britain at least originates with the anti-immigrant 1960s British politician Enoch Powell, to whom Kaufmann's associate David Goodhart has been compared (Shilliam 2018b). Kaufmann sees Powell's views as encapsulating both racism and 'racial self-interest'. His preference for excluding migrants over assimilating them may have made Powell racist. However, Kaufmann believes this should be separated from the 'genuine majority grievances buried in [Powell's] message'. According to Kaufmann, Powell was merely noting the rapidly changing nature of many of Britain's neighbourhoods and raising the valid point 'that the cultural impact of immigration is perceived as negative by most whites in reception areas' (Kaufmann 2018a: 319). Recall that this is what has been said much more recently of the perpetrator of the Christchurch massacre, Brenton Tarrant. So, in Kaufmann's view, racism can only be at work if it involves what the philosopher of race Jorge Garcia calls 'moral viciousness' (Garcia 1999). But it is 'not racism', he told *New Yorker* columnist Isaac Chotiner, if 'this idea of slowing down a rate of ethno-cultural change is … motivated by attachment to one's own' (Chotiner 2019).

The neighbourhoods Powell and Kaufmann were concerned about are the kinds described by British sociologist and anti-austerity campaigner Lisa Mckenzie. Mckenzie has written that 'white working-class women' living on housing estates already facing harsh austerity policies feared greater hardship as a result of asylum seekers being housed there (Mckenzie 2015). The vote to leave the European Union was not an expression of white working-class racism but one of 'precarity and fear' (Mckenzie 2016). However, as the demographers Danny Dorling and Sally Tomlinson reveal in their detailed analysis of the Brexit referendum results, the outcome could not be put down to the, albeit dominant, idea that 'the more deprived an area was, the more likely its residents were to vote Leave' (Dorling and Tomlinson 2019: 37). Furthermore, the fewer immigrants who lived in a given area, the more likely residents were to vote for Brexit, thus opposing the idea that the referendum was the result of interethnic tensions and downward pressure on scarce resources. The only determining factor swaying the vote was 'the personalities of those who led the campaigns' (2019: 26) and their success in fomenting fear of immigrants. The figurehead of the pro-Leave campaign, Nigel Farage, used a real photograph of migrants entering Slovenia to claim that EU membership is leading Britain to 'breaking point'. He thus pinned the blame for societal misery on migrants – and not even migrants actually entering Britain – rather than years of domestic austerity measures that have left poorer people from all ethnicities worse off. As many have pointed out, the manipulation of anti-immigration sentiment, openly aired across the media as a topic of legitimate debate, was a major catalyst for Brexit.

Kaufmann agrees that opposition to immigration gave birth to Brexit but posits that the only viable response is to assuage what he sees as legitimate fears by setting immigration levels 'that respect the cultural comfort zone of the median voter', also arguing in favour of Trump's Southern border wall (Chotiner 2019). Nadine El-Enany made the point early on that 'the racist discourse that has defined the Brexit campaign must be understood in the context of Britain's imperial legacy [and is] symptomatic of a Britain struggling to conceive of its place in the world post-Empire' (El-Enany 2016). This attention to the cultural meaning of loss of empire is utterly dismissed by Kaufmann when he reduces racism to a question of personal attitudes of warmth or hostility towards immigrants, measurable with online questionnaires. The detachment of racism from the racial regimes that continually play the bass notes under these debates is evident when Kaufmann wins points for asking 'inconvenient questions' that people who 'denounce everyone as racist' are said to dare not ask. Kaufmann contends that 'ethnotraditional nationalists' have a right to a secure white Christian tradition alongside those whom he calls 'vibrant minorities' and against those who refuse to assimilate into his vision of an elastic whiteness (Kaufmann 2018a: 28). He presents assimilation into whiteness as a question of individual choice. He completely ignores the extensive literature examining the circumstances in which once negatively racialized groups, such as the Jews or the Irish, 'became white' in US society, where they were positively counterposed to Black and Indigenous peoples (Brodkin 1999; Ignatiev 2015). By ignoring this history, which also has variants in other western countries, including the UK, Kaufmann is able to provide an intellectual justification for the increasingly widespread idea that beleaguered white people, reconstituted as coherent communities, have as much of a right as other 'identity-based' groups to protect their interests.

Kaufmann's context is Brexit and Trump's anti-migrant wall-building project. However, the detachment of what are commonly called 'open and honest debates' about immigration from racism, for which 'merely concerned citizens' are seen as wrongfully blamed, has been a feature of anti-immigrationism dating back to the 'gold rush'-era construction of the Asian 'yellow peril' in the US. A more recent example is the 2005 British Conservative Party's publicity campaign, which asked, 'Are you thinking what we're thinking?' under a pseudo-handwritten, lower-case: 'it's not racist to impose limits on immigration'. As Ben Pitcher correctly notes, the present-continuous 'thinking' is used knowingly in the place of the alternative 'believing' (Pitcher 2006). The billboard could not then be said to be an expression of a core party value. Rather, the message is that the party is in tune with the thoughts of the ordinary voter, who is a good person despite having doubts about the benefits of immigration. Over ten years later, the terms of 'not racism' have become more strident. While then there was a subtle granting of permission to be 'thinking' that the wish for more immigration controls was not racist, now there is open assertion that this is indeed so. Immigration has been successfully presented as 'not racism', and imposing restrictions on, indefinitely incarcerating, and deporting those who are labelled 'illegal' is just commonsense. Being anxious about immigration does not equate to being motivated by racism. Rather, the 'racial self-interest' of white identity politics is as rational as that of any other ethnic group. Given the centrality of white anxiety about immigration, not only to migration policy-making, but also to the manifestos of murderous white supremacists from Utøya to Christchurch, the blitheness with which the putative 'not racism' of anti-immigration is asserted is of concern.

Whiteness in 'white identity politics' is dislocated from its origins in the securing of racial supremacism over colonized and indigenized populations, obscuring the structures in which white people inherit the racially derived benefits denied to those racialized as non-white in Euro-American societies fuelled by the wealth of colonialism and slavery (Roediger 2019a). It negates the fact that whiteness was given meaning within racial regimes based on the theft of native lands and the enslavement of Black people. Whiteness itself is property, as noted in Chapter 1. It has intrinsic value as a quality that only white people can possess (Harris 1993; Moreton-Robinson 2015). The benefits that accrue as a result of being white come to be expected by white people, so that any threat to their status or their reputation is perceived as illegitimate, particularly when it comes from the racially subjugated. While Harris's theorization of whiteness specifies the US context of Indigenous dispossession and African enslavement, the globalization of white supremacy across the settler colonies, through the imbrication of Europeanness in whiteness, and as reproduced in contemporary migration regimes, makes this a useful framework beyond the US. It explains the claim that those who espouse a white national 'ethnotraditional' identity feel justifiably anxious about sharing finite resources with both new and older migrants who are, to use C.L.R James's formulation, *in* but not *of* the nation. Whiteness cannot be detached from its primary role of setting the boundaries of racial distinction and therefore it cannot be made to appear as just another among an array of ethno-cultures.

Whiteness cannot be detached from its primary role of setting the boundaries of racial distinction and made to appear as just another among an array of ethno-cultures.

To identify whiteness is to name racialized power. However, white people often hear this as a naming of themselves as individuals, rather than as beneficiaries of a system that they could contribute to dismantling for the benefit of everyone. That is why it is so common for white people to dislike being called white. Calling someone white is heard as akin to calling someone racist. To make this association is to be 'anti-white'. And this 'new racism' is seen as dominant in a world where anxieties about white demographics reign. Demonstrating the extent to which there is discomfort about naming whiteness, in April 2019, the British Channel 4 newscaster Jon Snow was investigated by the UK's communications regulator Ofcom for saying of a Brexit rally that he had 'never seen so many white people in one place' (BBC News 2019). The regulator received 2,644 complaints about his remark, which led to an official apology from Channel 4. These fears about the 'last days of a white world' grow with the increasing acceptability of the idea of 'white genocide' beyond the fringes of the extreme right wing from where they originate (Richmond and Charnley 2017).

The recalibration of white as one among a series of ethnic identities and 'anti-white racism' as a consequent possibility has antecedents in what Martin Barker called the 'new racism' in his book of the same name (Barker 1982). We can draw a line from Barker's discussion of the adoption of the pseudoscientific ideas of ethology and sociobiology in the late 1970s by the anti-immigration British Conservative Party of Margaret Thatcher to the idea that what Kaufmann today calls 'racial self-interest' is not only rational but also natural. Migrants to Britain were deemed incompatible with what Kaufmann openly calls white Christian culture because its 'bioculturalist' view of the world synthesized 'nature and culture, biology and history' (Gilroy 2001: 33). Migrants, in this vision, have been uprooted from their purportedly organic homelands and replanted in an inhospitable and alien climate. To repatriate them not only benefits white people motivated by 'racial self-interest' but migrants themselves also. This version of events is core to the 'great replacement' theory cited by the Christchurch terrorist. In Kaufmann's narration of legitimate white anxiety, biology plays a lesser role than psychology. Assimilation into what is portrayed as a superior white culture, whose ability to shift and accommodate difference is portrayed as its strength over others, takes the place of repatriation. But both the 'new racism' and Kaufmann's 'whiteshift' theory treat racism similarly.

Tapping out a constant rhythm above these narratives of 'not racism' is the implantation of Islamophobia into mainstream political culture. The widespread accept-ability that, because 'Islam is not a race', it is 'not racist' to question Islam and fear Muslims is crucial for understanding the widespread acceptability of figures such as Kaufmann, Goodhart, and Goodwin, whose study of national populism also couches it in terms of 'not racism' (Goodwin 2018). The mantra 'Islam is not a race' permits Islamophobia to flourish under the guise of concern for women and gay rights, and for a secularism rebranded as radical opposition to Islam and Muslims. The mushrooming of anti-Muslim racism under the guise of anticlericalism is a linchpin of the 'new atheism' movement. It is not immaterial that one of its central protagonists is Richard Dawkins, whose 1976 book *The Selfish Gene* was key to the theorization of sociobiology, an accelarated Social Darwinism of the post-war migration era which underpinned the 'new racism' and greatly influenced the political outlook of then British Prime Minister Margaret Thatcher (Dawkins 2016 [1976]). Kaufmann and Dawkins find a common home at *Quillette*, which Dawkins described as a 'superb online magazine [that] stands up for the oppressed minority who value clarity, logic and objective truth'.[6] It is more accurately a voicebox for white identity politics and racial pseudoscience wrapped in the fiction of 'viewpoint diversity'.

In the next chapter, I argue that 'not making it about race' is an impetus on the left as much as on the right of politics. An underlying core belief unites those on both sides: that race is made to matter too much.

3

Making It about Race

That bad calls are made in the name of identity is no
news to anyone. The question is whether those bad calls
(whether hypervigilance over microaggressions or, more
egregiously, policing of gender borders) are endemic to
this thing called identity politics or merely endemic to
all politics. God knows plenty of bad calls – and more –
came out of and continue to come out of those forms of
politics we deem *not* identity politics.

> Suzanna Danuta Walters, 'In Defence of Identity
> Politics' (2018: 482, emphasis in original)

In September 2018, the, since axed, Australian daily
satirical news show *Tonightly* ran a segment called
'Lefty Boot Camp' (ABC Comedy 2018). It opens with
a bearded white comedian, Jazz Twemlow, sitting in a
leather armchair. 'Hello,' he says, 'I'm left wing.' Being
left wing, he explains, means not taking too kindly to
the rise of the 'Alt-Right', who have 'somehow gone
mainstream, gaining a rock-and-roll, anti-establishment
vibe. But there's nothing very rock-and-roll about a
bunch of white men hating multiculturalism.' Then,
Twemlow continues, 'What is more interesting is who is

to blame for making neo-Nazis look like the new rock-and-roll punk, and the answer is, unfortunately, partly us.' The left's problem, according to Twemlow, lies with those who insist on pointing out racism. Brexit, for example, was the fault of those who insisted on 'slagging off' 17 million members of the UK population by calling them racist and failing to put forward a positive agenda: 'Yelling raciiiiiist online made us feel good about ourselves and had no long-lasting side-effects.' For Twemlow, the left replaces dialogue and debate with name-calling. He interviews an academic who says, 'I think that if you call a bunch of people sexist or racist, but they don't believe they are sexist or racist, all it's going to do is get them to rally around their own tribe. ... I mean how would you feel if I said, you're entrenched in white privilege?' The clip ends with Twemlow alternately donning yellowface and dressing as Hitler doing yoga: 'Remember, calling someone racist isn't going to unracist a racist.' Antiracists have been doing antiracism wrong.

While 'Lefty Boot Camp' is far from original, it summarizes a popular view that a 'reduction' of complex political issues to questions of race, gender, and sexuality is unhelpful and alienating. The virality of the video spoke to a belief on 'the white left' that it has ceded irony to the right and that progressives lose by taking themselves too seriously, as though all that was missing in the fight against racism was better jokes. This view twists Twemlow's repetition of racist tropes for a white audience into 'a punch at power' (Razer 2018). However, this wishful thinking negates the fact that it was overwhelmingly people of colour and antiracists who criticized the sketch, explaining how it served white supremacist aims by casting racism as an unhelpful explanation.[1] I refer to 'the white left' to suggest that 'not all white people' are the agents of white supremacy (Aouragh 2019: 11), although I share Daniel C. Blight's insistence that there can be no antiracism that is grounded in white identity (Blight 2019). Referring to 'the white left' makes it clear that Twemlow and other critics of 'identity politics' actually use the label 'the left' only to refer to the proponents of social justice whom they see as thwarting leftist aims.

Encapsulating the left's problems in 'Internet call-out culture', as this comedy sketch does, reveals a profound lack of engagement with the actually existing challenges presenting themselves to antiracists. Twemlow's thesis is inspired by Angela Nagle's book on the 'online culture wars', which argues that a 'deep intellectual rot in contemporary cultural progressivism' that she observes among users of the Tumblr website is responsible for the failure to beat the alt-right (Nagle 2017; see also Harman 2018). In these digitally mediated times, splits on the left are arguably exacerbated by white complaints against antiracist projects that receive disproportionate exposure and generate distraction. The lack of interest in the multiple histories of antiracism, which also differ widely between locations, leads to the struggle against racism being caricaturized and antiracists having to spend significant energy challenging damaging stereotypes of the type the 'Lefty Boot Camp' sketch exemplifies. Because antiracism has rarely been subject to serious study, being 'consigned to the status of a "cause", fit only for platitudes of support or denouncement' (Bonnett 2000: 2), there is very little understanding of the movement's diversity. Disagreements abound, but it is a stretch to hold them responsible for the failures of 'the left' to make political gains. It may be more fruitful to ask why 'the white left' so often fails to think race matters.

The demand on 'the white left' to stop playing the conceptual 'race card' and alienating white publics reveals how race functions to hide whiteness. Race is attached exclusively to minoritized groups whose presence within the nation is questioned. By conceptualizing racism as irrational, western societies largely conceive of themselves as antiracist or non-racist. This assumption allows calls for the construction of the discourse on race to coalesce around 'open and honest debates' that posit, as Angela Nagle did, 'the left case against open borders' (Nagle 2018) or whether Australia should curb immigration, as a debate held barely a week after the Christchurch massacre was framed.[2] The white innocence which these questions imply, as Gloria Wekker writes, allows for racism to become 'cemented and sedimented' while at the same time being declared 'missing in action' (Wekker 2016: 3). To bring race in is thus seen as an overreaching for a racialized perspective when things are 'more complex'. In fact, to refuse to see race is to choose simplicity and ignores the layers of power in and resultant complicity required in dealing with what race continues to do.

The rest of this chapter looks at how the question of race's explanatory helpfulness, or lack thereof, animates discussions of issues such as migration, Islamophobia, antiblack racism, and Indigenous sovereignty. I assess how doing antiracism is impacted by an analytically white framing of this adjudication of helpfulness. The recited truth that antiracism – re-labelled and dismissed as 'identity politics' – is responsible for elevating an anti-material and superficial recognition-based politics over a universalist – and, it is intimated, a more serious – politics of class plays a role in disabling race-critical analyses that foreground the imbrication of race in capitalism and the state (Goldberg 2011; Robinson

1983). By focusing on how themes of moralism, equivalence, and the perceived cul-de-sac of identity circulate within these political perspectives, I draw attention to what is lost when race is deemed useless.

Smugs versus ordinaries

The reason why the 'Lefty Boot Camp' worked comedically for many was because it spoke to the feeling, expressed by other white people, that 'you don't convince people by abusing them' (Sparrow 2013). Antiracism is seen as imbued with a moralism that blames individual voters for racist policy-making (Tietze 2014). Moralism was a touchstone of the pre- and post-Brexit debate in the UK and the Trump election in the US. Racism is portrayed by 'white left' writers as a middle-class stick to beat the working class with. 'Whenever working-class people have tried to talk about the effects of immigration on their lives,' wrote socialist Lisa Mckenzie, 'shouting "backward" and "racist" has become a middle-class pastime' (Mckenzie 2016). It matters little that 'whether it is Brexit, Trump or the French Front National, this kind of vote comes for the most part from the (lower) middle class, and the middle class' who are more likely to vote than the working class of any ethnicity (Winter and Mondon 2019).

According to Eric Kaufmann, a 'left-modernism turned moralistic and imperialistic' (Kaufmann 2018a) and backlash against the 'perfectionist creed of multiculturalism' (Kaufmann 2018b) were triggers for Leave and Trump voters. In his version of history, 1960s US social justice protests quickly descended into 'a frontal assault on intellectual merit and the norms of rules-based deliberation', resulting in the trumping of 'evidence and logic' by protest, 'emotional release', and 'moralistic poses' (Kaufmann 2018b). This opprobrium for the negative influence of 1960s counter-culture on what is presented as the true Socratic mission of the university is shared by Columbia University Professor Mark Lilla, for whom a 'moral panic about racial, gender and sexual identity' stunts liberalism's ability to govern and obscures such 'perennial questions as class, war, the economy and the common good' (Lilla 2016). Australian Marxist writer Jeff Sparrow sees what he calls a 'delegated politics' that replaces the direct protests of the 1960s as responsible for the institutionalization of a 'leftism embedded in various professional settings', such as universities, thus detaching the concerns of the left from their roots in the working class. The right-wing anti-political correctness of the 1980s could easily be tapped into by politicians among those whom Sparrow calls 'ordinary people' fed up with the sneering, 'smug politics' of these newly institutionalized elites (Sparrow 2018: 95).

Two racially coded sides – smug and ordinary – gather together simplified bundles of political interest. Sparrow's narration of the move from the streets to the campus recites a lament for the reduction, as he sees it, of leftist demands to 'achievable goals' such as the inclusion of Black and other ethnic studies in the curriculum (Sparrow 2018: 30–1). He does not see 'ordinary people' as benefiting from the capacity of ethnic studies to 'unsettle the normativity of the white academy', as Black Marxist Cedric Robinson saw it (Osuna 2017). The radical scholarship that wedged its way onto the US campus, is still being fought for elsewhere (Andrews 2018; Shilliam 2018a), and is far from secure even in the US (Osuna 2017), can only be seen as irrelevant for 'ordinary people' if race is seen not to concern them (Mitropoulos 2007). The Black radical historian Robin Kelley notes how, although the way in which 'the fire this time' – the time of Black Lives Matter – spread from town to campus recalled the historical pattern following the Harlem and Watts rebellions of the 1960s, its 'size, speed, intensity, and character' were noteworthy. Black students led 'coalitions made up of students of color, queer folks, undocumented immigrants, and allied whites' to fight the police brutality that targets Black people in the US, who, after all, are ordinary people too (Kelley 2016).

My intention is not to glorify student activism, some of which surely focuses on the narrow project of 'making the university more hospitable for black students', and not enough on how to 'become subversives in the academy, exposing and resisting its labor exploitation, its gentrifying practices, its endowments built on misery, its class privilege often camouflaged in multicultural garb, and its commitments to war and security' (Kelley 2016). However, it should be possible to criticize the conditions created by the American academy, and the neoliberal university more broadly, that individualize aspiration and police radicalism without seeing that as originating in the idea of Black studies or with radical Black scholars holding out against these systems. That is not to say that Black and other ethnic studies in the US have not been co-opted and commodified, more or less successfully. As Charisse Burden-Stelly shows, Africana studies 'was formed to fundamentally challenge the statist and imperialist logic of the traditional disciplines in the academy by focusing on redistribution; African and African descendant struggles for liberation and self-determination; and the importance of internationalism to the larger project of Black freedom' (Burden-Stelly 2016: 157). The fact that it quickly took on what she calls a 'culturalist' bent that moved it from materialist analysis to the humanistic disciplines should rightly be understood as part of the US Empire's ability both to accommodate and to discipline 'challenges to Eurocentrism, Euro-American coloniality, and white supremacy' (2016: 158). Therefore, while we can never discount individual agency in the move to institutionalization, it is important to read the story of Black studies against race as a structuring force.

The failure to see race as central rather than as peripheral to analyses of sociopolitical structures is what conjures the caricatures of the smug/ordinary binary. Beyond all other topics, race, and especially race intersecting with gender and sexuality, is the fault line that separates the 'plain speakers' from the 'out of touch'. The codification of race within terms such as 'ordinary people' and 'smug elites' defies the reality in which those most likely to be living in hardship in societies such as the US, Australasia, or Europe are Black, Brown, Indigenous, or of migrant origin (Shilliam 2018b). The historian of race and class David Roediger recalls that while writing his book *How Race Survived US History* in 2008, he kept a Post-it note with '7×' written on it to remind himself that 'that was then the ratio both of white wealth over Black wealth as well as of Black male prime-of-life incarceration rates over those of white males of the same age', the latter of which has since increased (Roediger 2019b). Despite Lisa Mckenzie's tweeted declaration that 'I also don't think race is central I think class is',[3] by setting racism up as a middle-class concern and economic hardship as a 'white working-class' one, she refuses the fact that austerity has on average had a worse effect on Black people and ethnic minorities in Britain than on the rest of the population (O'Hara 2014). Black people,

The desire to silence
talk of race with the
aim of encouraging
greater interethnic unity,
while commendable in
theory, is impossible if
it involves the denial of
facts.

migrants, and people of colour are thus excised from an ethnicized vision of the working class as white (Shilliam 2018b). As the sociologist of gender Alison Phipps has remarked, it is better to talk about 'working-class and white' people than to suture the working-class experience to a mythical vision of ethnic whiteness (Phipps and Lewis 2019). The desire to silence talk of race with the aim of encouraging greater interethnic unity, while commendable in theory, is impossible if it involves the denial of facts. Yet these facts are drowned out when talk of race is heard only as an *accusation* of racism rather than a critical analysis of how racialized power structures operate through class, nationality, citizenship, and gender (S. Hall 1980). Can we see a way to admitting how racial rule is predicated on the creation of 'white advantage' (Roediger 2019b), and thus on white complicity, without it being heard as calling white people 'racist and misogynistic uneducated losers' (Arruzza 2016)?

Lost honour

In March 2019, Wolfgang Streeck, a 'pre-eminent economic sociologist' (Roos 2018), was interviewed in the *New Statesman* magazine on his view that a second referendum on the EU would tear British society even further apart (O'Brien 2019). Streeck's move, following the 2008 financial crash, from 'third way' German social democracy to a more Marxist inspired anti-capitalism has been accompanied by his growing alarm about the impact of migration on national well-being (Roos 2018). His anxiety about the power of a '*Marktvolk*' (market people) over the '*Staatsvolk*', the national public that governments should first be

102

answerable to, evokes antisemitic 'conspiracy theories favoured by the alt-right' that equate transnational financial elites with a people whom, as Adam Tooze remarks, they quite simply do not represent (Tooze 2017). Streeck repeats the anti-immigration right's theory that immigrants are incompatible with western societies by startlingly claiming, 'If you had no borders, you could have no collective property belonging to a society ... would you want Nelson Mandela to be a refugee in Germany? No! He'd be a mail carrier bringing Amazon parcels to your house ... he was needed somewhere else' (O'Brien 2019). Leaving aside the assumption that an African migrant can do nothing but work for a labour-exploiting, tax-avoiding trans-national company, online radical theory and history archive Libcom pointed out that the suggestion that Mandela was solely responsible for the anti-Apartheid movement strikes from history the fact that the ANC was a mass movement.[4]

Streeck, like many on the nativist left, sees the political world through the looking glass. In this world, those whom Streeck calls the 'dishonoured' working class, or whom others refer to as the 'left behind' of economic globalization, are stifled by the orthodoxies of antiracism imposed by aloof cosmopolitan urban elites. Using the well-worn language of contrarianism, Streeck said, 'If everyone is of the same view in the room, I begin to feel uncomfortable' (O'Brien 2019). Speaking up against the unfettered migration of his imagination is speaking truth to power in a remarkable reversal of the world as seen from the actual members of the – Black and Brown – working class. Streeck's critique of capitalism cannot be disentangled from two interrelated positions he takes: the first, against open borders, is a factor doubtless motivating his joining the left-nativist, anti-immigration *Aufsetehen* platform, established as a left-wing answer to the virulently anti-migration and Islamophobic *Alternative für Deutschland* party (Weisskircher 2018); the second is his admitted failure to, as he puts it, 'warm up to identity politics' (O'Brien 2019). Streeck's increasingly extreme pronouncements on the negative effects of migrants and refugees, whose short-lived welcome to Germany he sees only through a lens of Germany's 'chronic hunger for labour' (Streeck 2016a: 2), cannot be disentangled from his belief that identity politics are 'synonymous with consumerist society' (O'Brien 2019).[5] The co-constitutive effect of these two positions could be seen in his post-election analysis of 'Trump and the Trumpists' (Streeck 2017).

The vote for Donald Trump, for Streeck, was a cry for help of a 'dishonoured' working class. He admonishes a centre left, enamoured of globalization and cosmopolitanism, and too ready to champion the rights of racialized and otherwise marginalized minorities to the detriment of 'ordinary people'. The centre left, he claims, has reaped what it has sown by abandoning 'the demobilized working class' in favour of 'ever new minorities [discovered] by experts and politicians' (Streeck 2017). These minorities, in particular the 'supply of low-skilled and low-paid service workers' he places outside the working class, have been unjustly prioritized over the 'silenced majority' that cannot be made to fit into 'status groups' 'defined by color, gender, national origin, sexual identification and the like'. In Streeck's world, cosmopolitan urban 'neoliberals' are gleeful that Americans are 'shortly to become a "minority in their own land"' because they are unaffected by the pressures created by outsourcing and undercutting (Streeck 2017). He pits white against migrant workers, who are redrawn as a mere 'supply' for financiers, neoliberal politicians, and, presumably, hipsters. No effort is made to disentangle the exploitation of migrant workers from the concerns of racialized people themselves, as though there were a direct conduit from the campaigns of undocumented domestic workers, for example, to the right wing of the Democratic Party; as if a counterfactual migrant Mandela were responsible for Amazon's shoddy labour practices.

Streeck's perspective goes beyond that of the political theorist Nancy Fraser, which resists the nativist conclusions he draws. Her writings on Trump have been the object of particular interest in Germany, making readings of the US context available to other locations (Hamade and Fraser 2017). Fraser proposes that the incorporation of all but the most marginal of 'feminists, antiracists and multiculturalists' into the 'progressive neoliberal cause' by the Clinton campaign led to the victory of a politics of recognition over one of distribution, which, she argues, Trump abandoned. Instead, she claims, he proceeded to 'double down on the reactionary politics of recognition'. In this way, Fraser shifts the blame for Trumpism onto the nebulously defined progressive political realm (Fraser 2017). Similarly, for Streeck, an elitist antiracist orthodoxy crystallized in Hillary Clinton's presidential campaign and in her dismissal of Trump supporters as a 'basket of deplorables'. It is unsurprising that Streeck, who argues for a 'return of the nation' against the EU (Tooze 2017), shows complete disregard for the materiality of race, and is unable and unwilling to accept that racism and nationalism have always existed in a relationship of 'reciprocal determination' (Balibar 1991: 52). He brushes off the lived realities of mainly working-class, Black, Brown, Latinx, and Indigenous women, men, and gender-diverse people. ('Transgendered restrooms infuriated everyone except those seeking access to them', he mocked.) His irritation with Clinton's emphasis on race and gender to the detriment of his preferred colour-blind, class-based politics leads to the concerns of the Black and Brown workers being simplistically aligned, in his reading, with those of Clinton and her 'financial back[ers] on Wall Street and Silicon Valley' and her endorsement by celebrities such as Meryl Streep and Beyoncé (Streeck 2017).

It may have come, then, as a surprise to Streeck and Fraser, although certainly not to those who rejected the unempirical assertion of Clinton as an antiracist leader and pro-transgender trailblazer (K.-Y. Taylor 2016), when in November 2018, in a *Guardian* series on 'the new populism', Clinton said, 'I think Europe needs to get a handle on migration because that is what lit the flame' (Wintour 2018). Clinton urged European leaders to send out a stronger signal that they were 'not going to be able to continue to provide refuge and support'; in other words, a call to close the borders. These declarations make it clear that the tendency, displayed by Streeck and others, to confuse pseudo-'woke' references with a real commitment to hard-fought antiracist principles, and, worse, the collapsing together of actual antiracists, such as Black Lives Matter activists, and neoliberal political leaders is an erroneous one. Streeck would probably not be interested in Black socialist scholar Keeanga-Yamahtta Taylor's analysis of the Black Lives Matter movement five years from its birth. In it she notes the divergent opinions among different actors in the movement about whether or not to attend a 'closed-door meeting at the White House in February of 2016' (K.-Y. Taylor 2019b). There was no simple equation of antiracism with Democratic politics. Clinton and Streeck clap to the same rhythm on migration and borders, both with a nod to the imagined spectre of the refugee as terrorist. As Streeck has made no bones about saying, '[T]he migration of the violence ... is destroying the stateless societies of the periphery into the metropolis, in the form of "terrorism" wrought by a new class of "primitive rebels"' (Streeck 2016b: 73).

Streeck rejects identity politics because, by seeing them as consumerist, he fuses them together with unfettered global capitalism, which in turn is made synonymous with open borders. This is concerning because his influential voice contributes to an erroneous view of national resources as finite, only justifiably shareable among members of the (white) nation. Such a view ignores the 'colonial matrix of power' determining relations between western and majority-world regions (Quijano and Ennis 2000). Although Streeck claims to believe that an end to capitalism will only come from below (O'Brien 2019), he displays a complete lack of interest in what that 'below' looks like. He cannot imagine that the concerns of refugees and migrants to Germany or African-Americans, Latinos, and LGBTIQ people in the US *are* the concerns of the working class, or that their struggle may, in the words of the Combahee River Statement, lead to everyone becoming more free: 'If Black women were free, it would mean that everyone else would have to be free since our freedom would necessitate the destruction of all the systems of oppression' (The Combahee River Collective 1977).

Misplacing identity

The Combahee River Statement, written by the Black lesbian socialist members of the Combahee River Collective (CRC), has become a touchstone of left-wing accounts of how identity politics went wrong. The CRC coined the term 'identity politics' to emphasize action by Black women who 'were radicalizing because of the ways that their multiple identities opened them up to overlapping oppression and exploitation'. The members of the Collective 'looked to "extend" Marxist analysis to incorporate an understanding of the oppression of Black women ... as an oppressed group that has particular political needs' (K.-Y. Taylor 2019a). The *political* in the slogan 'the personal is the political' was as important as the *personal*. The statement uncovers how a universalizing drive, particularly when mobilized by white feminists, and the left more broadly, leaves race out of the picture: 'We are not convinced ... that a socialist revolution that is not also a feminist and anti-racist revolution will guarantee our liberation... . [W]e know that [Marx's] analysis must be extended further in order for us to understand our specific economic situation as Black women' (The Combahee River Collective 1977).

For many critics, identity politics have been subverted by those with radically opposing politics to those of the CRC. The 'identity' in identity politics is said to be misconstrued as based on 'something "authentic" – one's skin-colour or membership of a specific group – rather than on ethical, historical and social affinity' (Aouragh 2019: 18). I do not disagree that there is often a lack of knowledge of the history of antiracism on display in contemporary social justice discourse. This was a topic of discussion on a podcast produced by Black British writer Reni Eddo-Lodge on 'political blackness', the umbrella term for people from different migrant groups which was in use within British antiracism until the 1990s. She interviewed both older and younger antiracist activists. Angelica, a member of Black feminist group Sisters Uncut, remarked that 'for a lot of people I think of our generation ... they are so adamantly against the idea of political blackness and they think it's like insulting, it's offensive. ... I appreciate what it was at the time.' For Black British Labour politician Diane Abbott, who was an antiracist activist in the 1980s, the 'backlash' she believes there is against political blackness today is unfounded. In her view, political blackness was emblematic of a spirit of collectivism born of shared struggle. She suggests that today, 'Hindus saying we're not Muslim and Muslims saying, well we're not Hindus and then even in Africa you had people from Northern Nigeria saying we're Hausa, we're not black, and you got Yorubas saying we're Yoruba, and you got Igbos saying we're Igbo', is in part due to a lack of knowledge of antiracist history (Eddo-Lodge 2018).

Nevertheless, I worry that the emphasis on this lack of historical knowledge and what is seen as the stress placed on intractable differences over commonality among antiracists today, which can largely be found among students and younger academics, is often overstated. Does too much emphasis on everything that is wrong with an inconsistent version of identity politics not risk missing the fuller picture when it comes to the struggle against racism? As my friend and comrade Gavan Titley once put it to me, 'Can you imagine asylum seeker movements tying themselves up in knots about the rights and wrongs of identity politics?' With this in mind, I want to ask, what if talking about identity politics as a distraction from antiracism were not *itself* a distraction from antiracism? Asking this would lead to an inter-rogation of some of the issues raised by the debates on identity and how they influence the question of what race does as an instrument of power and stratification.

Making It about Race

One figure who has published a book about the problems with identity politics is *Viewpoint Magazine* editor Asad Haider, for whom a 'mistaken identity' disrupts effective organizing around race and class in the US today (Haider 2018a). I propose to consider Haider's 2018 book *Mistaken Identity* because it is representative of a body of work that engages a serious critique of identity politics while foregrounding a materialist account of race (Aouragh 2019; Kumar et al. 2018). Haider's contribution is worth taking seriously because it sets out to avoid the colourblind pitfalls of postracialism. However, its attempt to present a new universalist politics that goes beyond the narrow choice of race or class ends up nostalgically replaying lost political opportunities, symbolized by the Haitian revolution and the 1960s US Black liberation movement, and mapping the narrow experience of the US activist scene onto the heterogeneous antiracism movement beyond its borders. Yes, we need to understand our antiracist history, but we must be careful not to mythologize what was after all a past replete with its own conflicts.

Frustration with the limitations of identity politics is a key dimension of the question 'What's the use of race?', or, in the terms of this book, 'Why does race matter?' Haider sees race as a categorical distinction that is created by the ideology of racism (Haider 2018a; see also Fields and Fields 2012). Race is thus of no use as 'a foundation for political analysis' because it 'reproduces this ideology' (Haider 2018a: 44). This view of race as having been created out of ideological racism differs substantially from the one I have been presenting in this book: that race itself is a technology, rather than a category, that pre-exists the idea of a taxonomical system of biological 'races'. Race, from this perspective, should be understood as a project and a process

110

elaborated by regimes such as colonialism and slavery and within which structures and ideologies take shape over time (Wolfe 2016). Racial ideology, for Haider, reduces 'human culture to biology' (Haider 2018a: 44). This misses the extent to which the biological is only one register in which race is played, as I have been arguing throughout (see also Stoler and Lambert 2014). To adequately critique the insufficiency of tightly bonded concepts of identity as a basis for political action, it is necessary to elaborate more profound accounts of how the instability of race means that it requires constant remaking. In other words, it is only by having a sophisticated account of how race works, which does not reduce it to the merely ideological, that we will be equipped to build the relational interpretations that can foster more productive alliances of solidarity.

In what follows, then, I examine Haider's problematization of what he sees as the excessive emphasis on victimhood and trauma in identity politics. This is portrayed as an obsession of contemporary social justice discourse. An examination of how it is treated in *Mistaken Identity*, and especially the connections Haider draws between movement politics and academic theory, leads me to ask whether the focus on these ultimately narrow debates may do more harm than good when it comes to the business of becoming more free, or, as the Italian-Ivorian trade union activist Aboubakar Soumahoro puts it, having 'the right to happiness' (Soumahoro 2019).

I ask what is lost when we fail to adequately explain how and why race matters in these discussions. I conclude the chapter by questioning the utility of a narrow US perspective on identity politics for antiracism in other locations that are nevertheless forced to exist in the shadows of its racial legacies.

Making It about Race

Pessimism or survival?

Part of the difficulty with the way in which 'identity politics' are discussed is that certain precise challenges within antiracism are conflated with the problem of organizing around identity per se. Haider suggests that antiracism today is far too concerned with the impact of historical trauma on racialized people in the present. This assumes that subjugated people have no capacity to resist the effects of trauma. Haider organizes his discussion of the negative impact of the language of trauma around his experience of the 2014 occupation at the University of California Santa Cruz. During the occupation, he claims, 'the race question already dominated everything' (Haider 2018a: 32). He proposes that discussions held among the occupation participants were steeped in an anti-material understanding of race as equivalent to trauma which construed people of colour as always victimized. In his description, this led to protesters being divided into people of colour, on one side, and whites, on the other. The former 'would focus on police brutality, ethnic studies, and postcolonial theory', while the latter got to take on 'the privatization of education and job insecurity' (Haider 2018a: 41). Reading this, I was hoping for a more fine-grained socio-logical analysis of how and why this split manifested. A social movements approach may have considered the roles played by the various actors involved and been better equipped to come to a conclusion as to whether it was the participants' identity alone that positioned them on either side of this split, or whether there were other factors in play. What would participants themselves have to say about Haider's observations? Instead of providing this viewpoint, Haider incongruously turns to a theoretical debate within Black studies to make

112

sense of what he sees as the narrow focus on trauma and victimhood and the detrimental impact that this has on antiracist organizing in the US today. According to Haider, the 'reactionary separatist' trend he witnessed in Black activism that relegated 'white "allies" last and "brown" people ... in the middle' is derived from the status granted to the 'pseudo-philosophy' of Afropessimism (Haider 2018a: 38).

More than any other branch of theory, Afropessimism has been held responsible for making US Black experiences incommensurate with those of any other racialized group. Whether or not this fully characterizes the approach taken by all scholars associated with the label, many of whom do not use it for themselves, is debatable. To briefly summarize it, Afropessimist thought sees Orlando Patterson's theorization of slavery as social death (Patterson 2018) as the abiding feature of African-American existence 'in the wake' of slavery (Sharpe 2016). The world since slavery, according to Afropessimism, is irremediably antiblack. Because, to cite its principal proponent, Frank Wilderson, Afropessimism 'seeks to "destroy the world" rather than rebuild a better one', the transformative or revolutionary aims of a previous generation of more radically aspirant students have been abandoned (Wilderson cited in Haider 2018a: 40–1).

The 'insistence on absolute negativity' in Afropessimism has been widely criticized from within Black thought itself. Lewis Gordon, for example, agrees that Black people face an objectively antiblack world, but he does not agree with the Afropessimists that the world itself is antiblack; an important distinction. To see the world as an 'antiblack racist project' is to see no point in attempting to remake it. For Gordon, this view of things renders Black struggle 'stillborn' (Gordon 2018a). In such a world, 'actual people with names, experiences, dreams and desires' are turned into 'vulnerable and threatening bodies' (Kelley 2016). The result, according to Gordon or Kelley, is disabling and individualizing, replacing a 'discursive, social, and relational' view of the human world with 'the non-relational, the incommunicability of singularity' (Gordon 2018a).

As we can see, then, Afropessimism at its most crude raises concerns. What I wish to interrogate here, though, is why a serious discussion of the problems around solidarity-building in US campus antiracism is conflated with a theoretical debate in Black theory. How does taking this approach add to a discussion of whether or not 'identity politics' have negatively impacted on the struggle against racism to the extent that they are suggested to have done by Haider and many others. In other words, while it is true that there is an 'increasing symbiosis between activism and academia' (Aouragh 2019: 5), we have to ask why debates that take place within universities have come to stand for problems in antiracism writ large. We might also ask where this leaves antiracists who are not students or academics.

Owing to the influence of Afropessimist thought, Haider contends, students are unable to envision more than the bare minimum of demands, appealing to a corporate university to furnish them with the accoutrements of ethnic studies: safe spaces and a decolonized curriculum. He believes this has caused them to give up on fighting for material issues which affect everyone, and arguably Black and Brown people more than anyone else, because the vicious cycle of interminable antiblackness means the fight is already lost. Haider worries that just when Black Lives Matter was showing the world the full extent of Black people's capacity to resist in the face of unspeakable violence, a discourse

114

that privileges Black trauma over Black agency received undue attention. It is not that Haider's discussion of the limitations of Afropessimism necessarily misdiagnoses a theoretical difficulty. The problem is that he makes unsubstantiated assumptions about the influence of heavily contested Afropessimist ideas on the multi-sited and often internally conflicted politics that go under the banner of Black Lives Matter and antiracism more generally. When it comes to student politics, much-maligned 'safe spaces' are most often straightforward demands for physical protection in an increasingly volatile and polarized environment. When universities allow extremists onto campuses in the name of 'academic freedom' or when students burn books such as that of Latina author Jennine Capó Crucet after her talk at Georgia Southern University in October 2019, 'safe spaces' are a modest and justifiable demand (Beckett 2019).

Given the anger and energy driving the Black Lives Matter protests, erupting with the 2012 acquittal of George Zimmerman, accused of the murder of Florida teenager Trayvon Martin, it is tenuous to claim that Afropessimist thinking was responsible for hijacking the radical potential of the movement. Yet that is what Haider intimates when he drastically expands his claim that Afropessimism had an intellectually disabling effect after the 2014 Ferguson uprisings that had activated Black Lives Matter protesters around the country. Haider states that Afropessimist language circulating on social media served 'as an ideological ballast for the emergent bureaucracies in Ferguson and beyond' (Haider 2018a: 40). A 'radical rhetoric of separatism' encouraged by Afropessimist thought 'and the reformism of the elite leadership' of Black Lives Matter, he claims, 'have converged to foreclose the possibilities of building a mass movement' (Haider 2018a: 41). However, there is little to prove that there is a direct link between the spike in interest in Afropessimist thought online and the problems of antiracist coalition-building, which have a longer and more complex history. And to call the grassroots Black movement in Ferguson a bureaucracy is also an imaginative stretch.

Haider's argument is part of a wider trend of identifying social media as a unique source of political challenges, from the links between 'Tumblr liberals' and the emergence of the alt-right drawn by Angela Nagle, to the assumptions about the origins of far-right extremism on the 'dark web' in the wake of the Christchurch massacre. The connections are rarely as direct as it is suggested. In the case of Black Lives Matter, the movement's history is generally narrated as having begun with a hashtag that emerged from a 'love letter' written by one of its founders, the Black activist Alicia Garza, and summed up in her Facebook status update of 13 July 2013: 'Black people I love you. I love us. Our lives matter.' Her friend and movement co-founder Patrisse Cullors put a hashtag in front of the words 'Black lives matter'. As Garza herself notes, of course, 'hashtags don't start movements, people do' (Scroggin 2016). Therefore, the extent to which BLM has been portrayed as a uniquely social media phenomenon should be treated with some scepticism (Freelon et al. 2016). People put their bodies on the line and were faced with the tear gas and rubber bullets of the trigger-happy 'Blue Lives Matter' police force with the backing of a largely antiblack public.

Nevertheless, Haider is justified in being concerned about the movement from the hashtag to the streets. He centres his criticisms on BLM 'representatives' who, spurred by social media, came to Ferguson following the protests in 2014. One such figure is Deray McKesson, then executive director of the educational not-for-profit Teach for America, an organization that promotes school privatization and opposes teachers' unions (Haider 2018a: 41). The role played by these social justice entrepreneurs is also criticized by Keeanga-Yamahtta Taylor in her five-year assessment of BLM (K.-Y. Taylor 2019b). And it is intimated in the documentary about grassroots activists in Ferguson, *Whose Streets?* (Folayan and Davis 2017). Therefore, it should not be discounted. However, it is not clear why Haider links these questions about the clash between the grassroots and platform politics with Afropessimist thought. He suggests that Afropessimist language provided cover for professionalized out-of-town activists. But the nature of the actual relationship between either Afropessimist thinkers themselves, adherents to the theory in university classrooms and online platforms, and the BLM spokespeople 'who got the most media play' is not made sufficiently explicit (Haider 2018a: 40). The reason why it is important to question the connections Haider draws is that it is precisely this type of fuzziness that lends itself to distracting from the important and necessary conversations that antiracists need to have.

There is plenty of evidence for the internal struggle within the Black Lives Matter movement over the involvement of figures such as McKesson. Activists on the ground at Ferguson, such as Darren Seals, who accused outsiders of 'hijacking the Ferguson movement' were not concerned by what discourse was used to do so (Kendzior 2016). Indeed, the words of Seals, who was found dead in suspicious circumstances in September 2016, like six other Ferguson organizers since (Dickson 2019), may well hit more Afropessimist notes than those of someone like McKesson. Seals believed that, 'if you are a black US citizen fighting for black rights, you are the underdog – up against a white supremacist system in which brutality toward blacks is legitimized and practiced, especially by police' (Kendzior 2016). Thus, because attacking 'identity politics', as we have seen throughout this chapter, has become so central to challenging the legitimacy of organizing against racial rule, we must be very careful to distinguish between contested theories and actual political practice. The extent to which the problems facing antiracism are due to bodies of thought and intellectual discussions, rather than the very clear and present threat of right-wing attacks, police infiltration, the criminalization of activism, and the top-down effort to co-opt and neutralize autonomous action, demands questioning. Why has so much airtime been given to academic arguments – in both senses of the word – about 'identity politics' when we could be working out solutions to exposing and ending racial oppression?

Furthermore, the suggestion that Afropessimist-inspired Black activism places too much emphasis on trauma and not enough on agency and resistance is called into question by Alexander Weheliye. Weheliye asks why we tend to equate freedom with western conceptions of humanity that see resistance and agency as central to what it means to be fully human. He is concerned that, in so doing, we risk overlooking the potential that human beings have for survival, which, although often barely perceptible, can be found even in cases of extreme 'depravation and deprivation' and in the places where humans have suffered most (Weheliye 2014: 39). Agency, resistance, and the neoliberal word 'resilience' are often mobilized to paper over the extent to which race is embedded in a Eurocentric conception of the human which divides between individual white subjects and a racialized mass of others. Weheliye looks instead for the instances in which, even when people appear to be utterly banished from the realm of humanity, their actions, no matter how small, signal the impulse that we all have for survival. This forces us to ask whether we find the political not by turning away from trauma but by looking intently at the potential for freedom therein.

Weheliye gives the example of the *Muselmänner* of the concentration camps, racistly named so because they were 'so ravaged by chronic malnutrition and psychological exhaustion that they resembled phlegmatic but still living corpses' (Weheliye 2014: 53).[6] The fact that, their near-death state notwithstanding, they expressed a yearning for freedom reveals the extent to which their '(in)humanity is survival' and is thus in itself political (Weheliye 2014: 121). As I now turn to discuss, it is only by failing to think critically about how it is a racial logic that establishes the criteria for what constitutes human action that we are left with a partial understanding of antiracism that highlights resistance and agency to the detriment of an observation of the minuscule, almost imperceptible, yet stealthily ever-present beating pulse of what Hortense Spillers calls 'the flesh' (Spillers 1987). As Audre Lorde wrote, the trauma of fear is a constant for those who live on its 'shoreline'. It is therefore 'better to speak remembering we were never meant to survive' (Lorde 1978).

It should not be that because some Afropessimists view race as a 'static ontology' rather than a political project – which because it was created under certain historical conditions can also be overcome – that race itself loses all capacity as a framework for analysing current social conditions and fighting against them. A

119

second problem, then, in Haider's *Mistaken Identity* is
to be found in his understanding of race. For Haider,
'race discourse engages in a regression of identity to the
biological, the biological disguised as the ontological
... rather than inscribed on the body by the chain, the
brand, and the lash' (Haider 2018b). However, the
inherent instability of race and the emphasis placed
in critical scholarship on race as project and process
clearly denotes that it is anything but an objective
marker of identity. W. E. B. Du Bois was clear on this
when he invoked the 'badge of race' that all those
who 'have suffered a long disaster and have one long
memory' are forced to wear (Du Bois 1940: 59). Race
is attributed, not chosen. It is therefore important to
distinguish between race as an analytical framework
and its subversion by either the radical anti-humanism
of Afropessimism, on the one hand, or the neoliberal
ventriloquy of antiracist activist discourse, on the other.
It is equally important not to conflate the two.

Far from race producing fixed categories, the need
under racial rule to constantly submit Black people to
disciplinary control exposes the intrinsic instability of
the very idea of race, which purports that each 'racial'
group coalesces around a 'natural' place in the world.
However, if there really was an equivalence between
race and identity, there would be no need to discipline and punish people with the lash, the prison, or
the constant tracking of Black life because everyone
would be in their 'natural' place. Thus, race must be
understood relationally as a process of racialization
that attaches to various groups of subjugated peoples
differently but which coheres in the service of white
supremacy (Harris 1993).

These interplays between race and identity are
parsed by Hawaiian scholar Kēhaulani Kauanui, who

distinguishes between race, indigeneity, and the study of Indigenous people. Kauanui remarks that,

> just as critical race studies scholars insist that race is a useful category that is a distinct social formation rather than a derivative category emerging from class and/or ethnicity, indigeneity is a category of analysis that is distinct from race, ethnicity, and nationality – even as it entails elements of all three of these. However, Indigenous peoples' assertions of distinction and cultural differences are often heard as merely essentialist and therefore resembling static identities based on fixed inherent qualities. (Kauanui 2016)

Indeed, a conflation of indigeneity with race has been at the heart of the evasion of material redress for racial-colonial rule in the settler colonial states and an erosion of hard-fought Indigenous political autonomy. In order to access a modicum of rights, Indigenous people have often been reduced to essentialized palimpsests of their past and forced to perform a cultural authenticity that in fact has been lost to many as a result of colonial dispossession. In Australia, the insertion of Aboriginal and Torres Strait Islander people into a multiculturalist framework means that it is very difficult in practice to attain the land rights enshrined in law by the 1993 Native Title Act. Communities litigating for rights to their ancestral lands are judged on whether or not they are able to demonstrate attachment to Aboriginal cultural practices, which in reality have been eroded by genocide, forced relocations, the mission system, and the theft of Aboriginal children under a policy of assimilation and racial 'improvement' (Moreton-Robinson 2015; Povinelli 2007; Wolfe 2016). On the flipside, child protection agencies are seen as hamstrung by so-called 'cultural baggage' when it comes to the protection of at-risk Aboriginal children. In reality, more Aboriginal children are being removed from their families today than at any other time in Australian history, often immediately after birth (Wahlquist 2018). In one public pronouncement on the dysfunction of Aboriginal families, social workers were described as being 'pressured to be "culturally appropriate"... "to the detriment of Aboriginal children"' (Bond 2018). These practices of racial rule are predicated on the still common belief that Indigenous cultures are not fit for the purposes of modern life. Indigenous demands for sovereignty thus centre on the right to a family life as well as the right to land.

Asad Haider, however, does not seem to have engaged with the writings of Indigenous scholars and activists on these and other topics. In *Mistaken Identity*, he conflates Indigenous sovereignty claims with the essentialist identitarianism of the 'race first' approach he claims to have witnessed at the UC Santa Cruz occupation. Haider could not fathom students' opposition to 'the very words *occupy* or *occupation*' (Haider 2018a: 33, emphasis in original; see also Kauanui 2016). The reduction of the term to 'celebrating the genocide of Indigenous people' was a 'stunning reversal of earlier academic fads', he claims (2018a: 33), although he does not elaborate on what these 'fads' were. Haider himself notes the 2011 Occupy movement's general failure to adequately address race because of its inability to 'take hold in the poorest neighborhoods' and 'diversify its ranks adequately' (2018a: 29). Therefore, his resistance to Indigenous people's objections to the meaning of Occupy are concerning. In fact, he compartmentalizes issues in exactly the same way that he accuses others of doing when they retreat into rigid identities by failing to consider Eve Tuck and K. Wayne Yang's insistence that, for many Indigenous people, Occupy is another settler re-occupation on stolen land. ... The pursuit of worker rights (and rights to work) and minoritized people's rights in a settler colonial context can appear to be anti-capitalist, but this pursuit is nonetheless largely pro-colonial. That is, the ideal of 'redistribution of wealth' camouflages how much of that wealth is land, Native land. In Occupy, the '99%' is invoked as a deserving supermajority, in contrast to the unearned wealth of the '1%'. It renders Indigenous peoples (a 0.9% 'super-minority') completely invisible and absorbed, just an asterisk group to be subsumed into the legion of occupiers. (Tuck and Yang 2012: 23)

Haider does not take into account the significance of the fact that 'indigenous dispossession was the historical precondition for Wall Street itself' (Kauanui 2016) and dismisses objections to the word 'occupy' as a signifier 'restricted to a single meaning traced back to Christopher Columbus' (Haider 2018a: 33). Singularly troubled by the racialized divisiveness of the UC Santa Cruz protests, Haider thus fails to consider that these conflicts take place within a context in which those of us who live on colonized lands continue to participate in the ongoing occupation of unceded sovereign country, a problem that is far from historical (Byrd 2011; Bhandar 2018; Kauanui 2016; Moreton-Robinson 2015; Wolfe 2016).

Taking Indigenous activists and scholars seriously would mean being unable to reduce their – wholly material – demands to mere victimhood claims. As Tuck and Yang point out, 'Land (not money) is actually the basis for US wealth. If we took away land, there would be little wealth left to redistribute' (Tuck and Yang 2012: 24). It is too easy from a settler perspective to reduce Indigenous people's demands to victimhood and performed trauma. Doing so means claiming dominance over Indigenous people, a position which should be untenable for those who wish antiracism to be grounded in the commonality of racialized people's struggles. Haider cannot in one breath admonish Frank Wilderson for denying the parallels between Black people in Ferguson and Palestinians under Israeli occupation,[7] and in the next reduce the demands of Indigenous people and their supporters to 'a debate that should probably have happened in a semiotics seminar' (Haider 2018a: 33). In fact, this puts Haider uncomfortably close to Wilderson, who denies the mutually constitutive nature of antiblack and anti-native racial rule in North America. According to Wilderson, although both antiblackness and colonialism are relational dynamics, they 'are secured by radically different structures of violence', thus making analogy and subsequent coalition impossible (Wilderson 2016).

This is where Haider's frustrations with race as a framework for understanding and resisting power and his complaints about the supposed dominance of the language of victimhood and trauma come together. As Indigenous people know, because they experience it every day, being told to 'just get over it' is a right-wing mantra repeated by the shock jocks and pundits of the Murdoch channels and tabloids and by intellectual proponents of the argument that it is time to 'move on' from the guilt of colonialism (Bruckner 2012; Ferguson 2004). In Australia, these arguments have been used in calls from government ministers to abolish sections of the Racial Discrimination Act.

It is not immaterial that this doubling down on the dismissal of the effects of centuries of racial domination comes at a time when, emerging from the haze of multiculturalist disappointment, more Indigenous and Black people and people of colour are talking about decolonization. From the calls to decolonize the curriculum by students in South Africa, the US, and the UK (Bhambra et al. 2018), to the rejection of the 'recognition' agenda by First Nations people in both Canada and Australia (Coulthard 2017) and the rise of a 'political antiracism' directly opposed to the 'moral antiracism' of 'the white left' in France (Bentouhami 2018), racialized people are resisting the terms of their participation as decided upon by liberal governance. It is not surprising, then, that they are met not only with 'white innocence' (Wekker 2016) but also, in these more openly racist times, with derision for 'playing the victim'; always a strategy for deflecting from demands for reparation, autonomy and sovereignty. Might it not be the case that what is interpreted as the overemphasis of victimhood and trauma is in fact the demand for Euro-American societies to face up to the ongoing effects of colonization, genocide, and slavery at a time of deep white crisis?

The problems of seeing the world from where you stand

The (re)turn to anticolonialism is grounded in the realization that the demands of racialized people for inclusion, acceptance, and recognition have largely failed. I think Asad Haider agrees, and he correctly diagnoses the limitations of assimilation and multiculturalism in his discussion of the struggle of religious Muslim women banned from wearing the veil since 2004 in France. However, the way he approaches this theme reveals that he is not aware of French antiracist politics, reading it instead from his vantage point on the US left. This is clear in the way he frames his discussion as a critique of 'liberal rights discourse' by imagining the campaign against the hijab ban as a timid request for social inclusion. Haider argues that fighting against the hijab ban should not be organized around 'a defence of the rights of Muslims'. He points out that emphasizing rights over freedom privileges 'the perspective of liberal tolerance [and] traps the Muslims it claims to defend within a victimized identity rather than joining them in a project of collective emancipation' (Haider 2018a: 104). However, to propose that French Muslim activists and their supporters frame their struggle around 'rights' reveals Haider's lack of knowledge of the realities of French activist debates. While this has been a feature of Muslim French campaigns against Islamophobia, it does not adequately describe the position taken by most activists, faced today with an onslaught of top-down discrimination, mediatized hate speech, and violence on the streets. Haider's mischaracterization results in a conflation of what he calls the 'liberal tolerance' perspective with the actual demands of anti-Islamophobia campaigners in France. It exposes the wider problem of imposing a narrow perspective on race, grounded in particular US debates, on the world in general.

Similar to his amalgamation of Afropessimist discourse and Black Lives Matter, Haider problematically juxtaposes French philosopher Alain Badiou's criticism of 'today's self-congratulatory discourse of moral responsibility and the ethics of military intervention' (Haider 2018a: 105) with Muslim French demands. Prominent transatlantic neoconservatives such as Bernard-Henri Lévy or former French Foreign Minister Bernard Kouchner, a proponent of western military intervention in Syria, are made to appear adjacent to the demands of Muslims and their supporters when Haider claims they mobilize a discourse of victimhood and appeal to the French state to recognize their rights. Haider, following Badiou, criticizes 'humanitarian interventionists' for seeing those on whose behalf they intervene as nothing but victims. However, campaigners against Islamophobia have nothing in common with these neoconservative ideologues. In fact, not only do French proponents of 'humanitarian intervention' have no concern for the rights of Muslims in France, they also have disdain for them, often supporting their outlook with racist statements about Muslims. For example, Lévy declared in 2006 that 'the veil is an invitation to be raped' (Pitt 2006). While he sees the Jewish head covering as a 'religious symbol,' the Muslim veil is 'a political emblem'. He has also criticized Green Party Senator Esther Benbassa for claiming 'that a miniskirt is no less alienating than a chador' (Lévy 2016). In a less offensive tone, Kouchner, while admitting that the ban on the hijab and the burqa would draw international criticism, said it was necessary for the sake of 'women's dignity' (*20 Minutes* 2010).

Far from being seen as victims, in reality, mainstream opposition to Islam casts Muslims as threats to French society and mores. France is presented as the real victim, forced to bear more than its fair share of the brunt of Islamic fundamentalism. No more clearly can this be seen than in the growing acceptance of the aforementioned discourse of 'anti-white racism', not only on the extreme- and centre-right, but also on the left, including among several leading French antiracist associations (A. Lentin and Titley 2011; Munier 2014; Vincent 2012).

Haider uses his misreading of a local case to make the theoretical point he actually wants to make about the primacy of victimhood in antiracist rhetoric. In his view, a discourse of victimhood has travelled from the identity politics margins to the right and the centre. Haider argues, following Wendy Brown, that the state's construction of rights in relation to groups perceived in terms of the 'particularities of their injured identities' is anti-emancipatory (W. Brown 1995; Haider 2018a: 105). Nevertheless, these claims require a much stronger grounding in the evidence, especially where the chosen example of French state Islamophobia is concerned. Indeed, French foundations for the need to take a strong stance against 'ostentatious religious coverings' have had recourse to many avenues of legitimation. But the signification of the veil in the context of France's defeat in Algeria – when France to this day continues to paint itself as the unjustifiably injured victim – is undeniable (Fanon 2007 [1965]). So, it is not possible to separate contemporary Islamophobia, ongoing settler colonial domination of Indigenous lands, or, indeed, racism more broadly from colonialism, not only in the past, but also today in the state's treatment of Indigenous peoples and those racialized as other than white. Race matters here because the assignation of victimhood is itself a racial-colonial determination; colonizers reserve the right both to reduce Indigenous, Black, or migrant demands to performances of victimhood and to cast themselves as victimized in the face of these demands. It is another example of the way in which political conflicts are made to work in and through race. In these debates, the marginalized are given roles and forced to play according to racial rules.

Haider concludes *Mistaken Identity* with a call for an 'insurgent universality' (Haider 2018a: 109). However, his arguments remain focused on particular political disagreements on the US left, so it is questionable whether they can form the basis for a new universalist politics unshackled by the false

Colonizers reserve the right both to reduce Indigenous, Black, or migrant demands to performances of victimhood and to cast themselves as victimized in the face of these demands.

universalism of Euro-modernity. If a major problem facing antiracism today is the mistranslation of local specificities across the accelerated times and flattened spaces of digital communications, we will not be better served by further contributing to the mapping of antiracism in the US onto other contexts. A view from the periphery might serve to temper the zero-sum mood that pessimism about the dominance of identity politics creates.

There is no golden era of antiracism, a time when it was not beset by internal conflicts around representation, respectability, or gendered hierarchies, and externally thwarted by paternalism, tokenism, or subsumption under the weightier concerns of class solidarity or universalist feminism. Today, at a time when the FBI has created a new category of crime – 'black identity extremists' – which criminalizes protesters who act 'in response to *perceived* racism and injustice in American society' (Blades 2018, emphasis added), separating something called 'identity politics' from social justice struggles in general might just be handing the right a language with which to further justify an increasingly repressive agenda. There is no equal fight between 'white identity politics' and race consciousness 'as a source of survival and support against a violent modern humanity committed to a "race" system' (M. White 2019). How we navigate conflict and division does not have to come at the expense of recognizing this.

As I now turn to suggest, the increased tendency for top-down condemnations of antisemitism to act as a proxy for antiracism means that a politics that is attentive to the structures and strictures of race is more urgent than ever.

4

Good Jew/Bad Jew

Hideous Jew Alana Lentin calls for open borders for
Australia.

Good work, Cora. The jew in its natural habitat, trying
to subvert countries from within by pleading for open
borders. The malice and insanity this race of hook-nosed
little shits have for us knows no bounds. Look at that
huge kike shnozz on her, too.
Posts on Vanguard news network, 29 July 2013[1]

On 8 March 2016, Michael Pezzullo, Secretary of
the Australian Department of Home Affairs, felt
compelled to defend the actions of his department
against criticisms of a 'contentious area of public
policy and administration', the mandatory and
indefinite detention of asylum seeker children. In
a press release, he noted, 'recent comparisons of
immigration detention centres to "gulags"; suggestions that detention involves a "public numbing and
indifference" similar to that allegedly experienced
in Nazi Germany; and persistent suggestions that
detention facilities are places of "torture" are highly
offensive, unwarranted and plainly wrong'. The use

of the term 'allegedly' drew the ire of commentators on social media, leading the Secretary to issue a correction. He was concerned to clarify his approach to the seriousness of the Holocaust, while halting any questioning of the morality of the Australian government's policy of indefinite mandatory detention for people seeking asylum. Lest there be any continued confusion that he condoned the Holocaust in any way, Pezzullo explained that 'to allege that the Nazi regime promoted indifference towards its abuses is bad history. ... The Nazi regime promoted racial hatred. Far from seeking to numb an indifferent public, it sought to vilify and persecute Jews and others, before engaging in the systematic and evil genocide of the Holocaust' (*New Matilda* 2016).

In Pezzullo's reading, it is 'bad history' to say that indifference accompanies an overt policy of ideological racism and a programme of mass genocidal extermination. But a key dimension of racial rule, as Fanon taught us (Fanon 1986 [1967]), is precisely the promotion of 'indifference to abuse' through the dehumanization of those in its sights and the disregarding of their exploitation, discrimination, incarceration, and ultimately death. The detention of thousands of asylum seekers in centres both within Australia and offshore has led to many deaths, including suicides and deaths from medical neglect. Detainees have been subject to physical, psychological, and sexual abuse. This ongoing situation is indeed made possible, at least in part, by what Pezzullo calls 'indifference' (Boochani 2018).

White Jews, in contrast to asylum seekers, and to Indigenous, Black, Roma, and Muslim people, have been hyper-humanized since the end of the Holocaust and the establishment of Israel. We have been pulled by both a western Christian establishment and the outstretched arm of the Zionist state into the Eurocentric and exclusionary borders of the human, a terrain which is always defined in racialized relation to the not-quite human and the non-human (Weheliye 2014). It is not the first time in history that Jews have been bestowed with humanization, a dubious gift which divides us from other non-Christians and non-whites. The emancipation of the Jews following the French revolution was experienced by the Orthodox Ashkenazi, who valued their autonomy over incorporation into the nation, as a 'revolution from above' (Traverso 1996). The expansion of the nation-state, liberal ideology, and colonial rule undergirded the post-revolutionary French state's need to domesticate the Jews (Katz 2018). This need was evident, for example, in the 1870 Crémieux Decree, which granted French citizenship to colonized Algerian Jews but not to Muslims. This formal inclusion in the body politic did not, however, erase the political antisemitism of the late nineteenth century, which mapped onto older forms of Christian Judeophobia (Judaken 2018; Postone 1980). Many Jews have also been willing participants in this integration into civilization, which meant giving up what we had in common with other racialized peoples; our shared 'barbarism' (Slabodsky 2015).

Today, the strategic significance of the state of Israel and its heavy promotion of a link between antisemitism and anti-Zionism, with the support of the official bodies of world Jewry and the majority of the world's states, means we must be careful about drawing analogies between the acme of social and political antisemitism in Europe and the present day. Nevertheless, the political antisemitism that is finding new levels of acceptability in the West is evidence of the tenuousness of the top-down humanization and exceptionalization of European Jews

– but not Arab or Black Jews – and the problems that arise when the majority of white Jews accept this state of affairs. Jews' participation in the whitening of Jewry weakens the line of defence against the coloniality that produced the notion of Jewish, and other, racial difference (Gordon 2018b).

The general failure to theorize antisemitism in relation to racial rule and colonialism (Judaken 2018; Slabodsky 2015), and the allied solidification of European cultural supremacy, reduces it to a cipher for performative outrage. Denunciations of racism are dismissed as soon as any association is made with the Holocaust, Nazism, or fascism. As I argued in Chapter 2, the function of freezing racism in ideal-typical examples from the past is to shield contemporary racists from accusation, thus freeing almost all but the Nazi genocide itself from the taint of racism. Expression of opposition to antisemitism functions as a ballast against denouncements of racism. In the present moment, publicly performing opposition to antisemitism and support for Israel – the two having been made equivalent – has also become a proxy for politicians and public figures' commitment to antiracism. Leaning on antisemitism as the *sine qua non* of racism and associating it singularly with the Nazi Holocaust, reinterpreted as a unique and aberrant event rather than the manifestation of a 500-year process, silences any questioning of this professed antiracism.

In April 2019, British Conservative politician Jacob Rees-Mogg mocked Black Labour Member of Parliament David Lammy for comparing the right-wing European Research Group he chairs with the Nazis, 'an organization and creed that killed six million Jewish people'.[2] Interviewed on the BBC by Andrew Marr, who has long shed his Maoist roots to become a mouthpiece for nativist discourses, Lammy pointed out that Rees-Mogg condoned Nazism by posting a video of the leader of the Islamophobic German *Alternative für Deutschland* party on his webpage and attending a dinner with the far-right Traditional Britain Group, which says that Doreen Lawrence, mother of murdered Black teenager Stephen, 'should be requested to return to [her] natural homeland' (Usborne 2013). In an attempt to distinguish the mainstream from the rightist fringes, Marr counters that 'it's a dangerous thing surely to accuse him [Rees-Mogg] of being close to Nazi ideology', adding that 'a lot of people would be absolutely outraged' by Lammy's suggestion that Boris Johnson is courting white supremacism by 'hanging out with Steve Bannon'.[3] The outrage of 'not racism' multiplies manifold when the aberrance of Nazism and white supremacism are evoked. While this performance is integral to the right and mainstream of politics, it also exists on the left. The British Labour Party under Jeremy Corbyn, which was embroiled in what was widely referred to as an 'antisemitism scandal' under his leadership, was defended by its supporters as the 'antiracist party', implying that antisemitism is no more than a right-wing smear (Goodfellow 2019).

The political utility of antisemitism today is not to illuminate the operations of race, but rather to obscure them. The severing of race, as a technology of rule, from 'frozen' accounts of racism has precipitated a public illiteracy about how race works that presents a serious challenge for antiracism. Race, understood throughout this book as a key technology of power, has largely been evacuated from mainstream discussions of migration, citizenship, class, and identity, not to mention policing, health, or education. In this chapter, I argue that a proxification of antiracism that can be observed in the current performative preoccupation with antisemitism obscures the workings of race further still. Therefore, to shed light on what is deliberately obfuscated, the question of antisemitism and its intense politicization must be explored to further answer the question why race still matters.

What is antisemitism and who is antisemitic, and why and to what ends antisemitism is named, are questions that have come to dominate political discussions on both sides of the Atlantic against a backdrop of white supremacist violence and accompanying apologetics. To be against antisemitism today is variably to uphold racial rule and to undermine it. These are not logically consistent positions and they necessitate disentanglement. Sorting out these strands can shed light on how antisemitism coheres with other forms of racism, particularly Islamophobia; how white supremacism and colonialism may be served by forms of anti-antisemitism; and how, in contrast, its denial and minimization from other quarters detract from the broad fight against racism. Whether antisemitism is tangible or a fictive weapon is a question and a fault line that slices in several non-linear directions, thwarting obvious answers. Antisemitism is both straightforwardly manifest in racist violence, both physical and discursive, and perceptible through the chimera of a shattered mirror (Langmuir 1993). It sounds warnings about the snares of complicity. Its usages and meanings reveal important lessons about the dangers of ordering racisms hierarchically against a backdrop of white supremacy.

Zoning in on antisemitism draws together the various components of this book: the resurgent fusion of race and genetics; the redrawing of the definitional boundaries of racism; and the dismissal of the 'merely cultural' as 'factionalizing, identitarian and particularistic' (Butler 1998: 33). It opens questions that are imbricated in the

The political utility of antisemitism today is not to illuminate the operations of race, but rather to obscure them.

racial; questions of nation, belonging, and loyalty, of the inextricability of race from the colonial, of what constitutes whiteness and white supremacy, and of solidarity and its absence. It is not coincidental that at this time of heightened white crisis, a time during which it seems we are teetering on the brink of fascism, antisemitism becomes a point of intense debate. If, as we have seen, the attempted genocide of the Jews of Europe is held up as the height of racism in practice, it is unsurprising that the extent of the crisis is discursively circumvented via a deflection that centres on whether antisemitism is present or absent in a range of contexts. Against both the weaponization of antisemitism in the service of the racial-colonial and its dismissal as a strawman hoisted by the right to stave off challenge from the opposing end of the political spectrum, as could be seen in the Rees-Mogg vs Lammy example, I conclude by arguing that a challenge to antisemitism that is attentive to the role it plays in racial rule points towards productive ways to decolonize and politicize antiracism in these critical times.

The co-dependency of antisemitism and Islamophobia

For a widening circle on the right and for many centrists today, the defence of Jews relies on the classification of Muslims and Islam as the world's greatest threat, and of Islamophobia as a bogus and illegitimate concept. The pitting of Jews against Muslims and of the racisms we each experience plays a central role in how antisemitism is presented as a problem on the rise today. To cite the aforementioned Bernard-Henri Lévy, 'the principal fuel of the new anti-Semitism, a fuel capable of stirring people up and rekindling the pogromist urge, is anti-Zionism' among Muslims. What he calls 'today's new alliance of Christians and Jews' has formed owing to the 'common and violent enemy' of Islam (Lévy 2017). But the vigour with which opposition to Islam and Muslims is legitimated depends on neglecting the fact that where there is antisemitism, there is very often Islamophobia also. Far from Jews and Christians being in natural alliance, in reality both Jews and Muslims are racialized as the intrinsic Other within; as inimical to the West and to Christian culture (Anidjar 2003). As we shall see, this is despite the fact that contemporary antisemitism often takes a 'philosemitic' tone that, while pitting 'good' Jews against 'bad' Muslims, can only do so while racializing and essentializing Jewish people (Bouteldja 2015).

The history of antisemitism, and the Holocaust primarily, is mobilized both in denial of 'real racism' and to shift blame for its perpetuation onto the proponents of what another French writer, Pierre-André Taguieff, referred to already in 2002 as 'the new Judeophobia', in his book of the same title (Taguieff 2002). Taguieff proposes that this form of Jew-hatred is dominant in the twenty-first century. In a similar vein to Lévy, he sees today's antisemitism as coming not from whites or from elites, but from Muslims and anti-Zionists. While Taguieff's position may have been novel in 2002, it has since become hegemonic. In his book, he couches it in a classist and racialized demonization of young people of North African origin in France. This has been a major theme since at least the 2002 French presidential elections, which saw the first near-win of the far-right *Front national* party. Subsequently, rising to a crescendo with the deepening of the War on Terror, the cementing of Islamophobia in mainstream policy, popular discourse, and political culture is shielded from

the charge of racism by making it about defending
Jews from antisemitism. Presenting Muslims and anti-
Zionists as the real antisemites allows the history of
the Holocaust to be cynically manipulated in order to
police Muslims and quell pro-Palestinian activism. This
is far from being unique to France.

Antisemitism is often dismissed or excused by
those who find common ground in Islamophobia. For
example, right-wing British philosopher Roger Scruton
was sacked from his role as housing adviser to the British
government in April 2019 after he supported the antisemitic conspiracy theory that the Jewish philanthropist
George Soros wields an 'empire in Hungary' during an
interview for the *New Statesman* magazine (Weaver and
Walker 2019). Scruton was a long-standing friend of the
Hungarian Prime Minister, Victor Orbán, who accuses
Soros and his Open Society Foundation of attempting
to undermine the Hungarian nation-state. Hungary's
anti-Soros hate campaign heralded an atmosphere of
increasingly brazen antisemitism. In October 2019, a
fifty-strong mob attacked a Jewish community centre
in Budapest, attempted to torch it, and covered the
building with neo-fascist slogans (Hume 2019). Rising
antisemitism in Hungary accompanies the virulent and
violent anti-refugee racism which saw the borders being
closed to those seeking asylum from the war in Syria in
2015. Government-funded billboards with a 'sneering'
picture of George Soros were accompanied by the
words, 'Let's not let Soros have the last laugh' and '99
percent reject illegal migration'. In this way, Jewish
'meddling' was presented as having been instrumental
in bringing 'Muslim invaders' to Hungary, as Orbán
described refugees in 2018 (Leifer 2018).

The campaign against Soros, which his son described
as 'dripping with anti-Semitism', reaches far beyond

Hungary. Although it begins on the extreme white supremacist 'anti-globalist' fringes, it extends into the political mainstream, where Soros is attacked for orchestrating attacks on the right, including false accusations of fomenting antifascist violence, via his support for progressive causes (Wilson 2018). In October 2019, Jacob Rees-Mogg described Soros as 'Remoaner funder-in-chief', making reference to his financial support for 'Best for Britain', an organization fighting to keep the UK open to EU membership. Despite the fact that the remark has clear antisemitic undertones, Lord Alfred Dubs, who had come to Britain on the Kinder Transport, apologized to Rees-Mogg for accusing him of taking a line 'straight from the far-right's antisemitic playbook' (Buchan 2019). This is revealing in a context in which Soros has repeatedly been the target of virulent antisemitism from the White House to the Hungarian streets, with Donald Trump, for example, claiming that Soros is 'paying refugees to illegally enter the country' (Levin 2018). While accusing Muslims and the left of antisemitism is par for the course, the right seems to play by different rules when it comes to its own antisemitism.

In Roger Scruton's case, he defended his allegiance with Orbán from any potential charge of antisemitism by relying squarely on Islamophobia. Hungarians, he claimed, 'were extremely alarmed by the sudden invasion of huge tribes of Muslims from the Middle East' (Eaton 2019). Supporting Scruton, the editor of the *Jewish Chronicle*, Stephen Pollard, accused *New Statesman* journalist George Eaton of 'grotesquely distorting' his comments, while hypocritically retweeting the 'antisemitic meme' that 'Isis learned a lot from Israel on how to build an expansionist state'.[4] Perhaps Pollard overlooks Orbán's antisemitism because Orbán himself swings between manipulating antisemitic tropes such as 'Hungary's enemies "do not believe in work, but speculate with money; they have no homeland, but feel that the whole world is theirs"' and accepting the World Jewish Congress's invitation to speak at its 2013 convention in Budapest (Zion 2018). During his speech there, 'Orbán not only denounced antisemitism, he also recognized the Jews as allies in his fight for international acceptance for his controversial policies' (Wertheim 2017: 277). Israel's Prime Minister, Benjamin Netanyahu, has also emerged as a key Orbán supporter, welcoming him as an ally in the fight against antisemitism and against the 'threat of radical Islam' which 'could endanger the world' (Zion 2018). This unveils the Israeli government's solidifying alliance with the European far-right under Netanyahu.

Stephen Pollard enthusiastically shared articles defending Scruton by *Spectator* magazine editor Douglas Murray and prominent ex-Muslim Maajid Nawaz for his column in the *Jewish News*. Pollard, editor of one of the world's oldest Jewish newspapers, appeared able to overlook Scruton's opposition to Soros despite its inherent antisemitism. He publishes articles by the journalist Melanie Phillips, one of the key intellectual proponents of the 'crisis of multiculturalism' thesis, whose writings in the 'fear of Eurabia' genre were collected in white supremacist Anders Breivik's 'compendium' on which he drew to justify the Utøya massacre of 2011. In a 2019 *Jewish Chronicle* column, Phillips downplayed white supremacism, arguing that, today, 'some Jews are now even joining the manipulative campaign to camouflage Muslim antisemitism and extremism by claiming the biggest threat to the world is coming from the far right' (Phillips 2019).

Douglas Murray and Maajid Nawaz, for their part, are on the frontline of the intellectual rationale for state-sponsored and popular anti-Muslim racism. In a stunning reversal of the actual experience of Muslims worldwide, Murray's 2013 book *Islamophilia* contends that 'metropolitans' are dangerously in thrall to an Islam that can do no wrong. His 2017 follow-up, *The Strange Death of Europe*, zones in on Muslim 'migrants raping and murdering and terrorizing', killing off an undefined European culture (Hinsliff 2017). The Quilliam Foundation, established by Maajid Nawaz on an Islamophobic agenda that demonizes Muslims, was essentially created to assist the UK government's countering violent extremism programme, Prevent, which it was paid a million pounds to promote (Kundnani 2015). Nawaz has been personally associated with Tommy Robinson/Stephen Yaxley-Lennon, the founder of Islamophobic street gang the English Defence League, who was jailed for nine months in 2019 'for seriously interfering with the administration of justice' (Busby 2019). In 2018, Nawaz and Quilliam were exposed by child sexual exploitation expert Ella Cockbain for cementing the narrative that Muslim 'grooming gangs' were disproportionately responsible for incidences of child sex abuse in cities in the North of England based on 'a case study in bad science' (Malik 2018).

What shielded Scruton from accusations of antisem-itism in the eyes of Pollard, Murray, and Nawaz was shared opposition to Islam and Muslims. Contrast their dismissal of Scruton's effective support for Orbán's antisemitic attack on Soros in the service of their shared Islamophobia with their opposition to US Congresswoman Ilhan Omar. Omar, the first Somali-born Muslim woman to be elected to office in the United States, is a religious Muslim who wears a hijab and whose outspoken remarks on Palestine, US imperialism, and the nefarious impact of the pro-Israel lobby on US politics became a flashpoint for discussions of what constitutes antisemitism today. Omar came under widespread condemnation for a tweet – 'It's all about the Benjamins baby' – which was interpreted as mobilizing the antisemitic trope associating Jews with money. When pressed for clarification, she claimed she was referring to the American Israel Public Affairs Committee (AIPAC), which brands itself as 'America's Pro-Israel lobby'. She later contextualized her remark by reaffirming the 'problematic role of lobbyists in our politics, whether it be AIPAC, the NRA or the fossil fuel industry'.[5]

In March 2019, Omar gave a speech to the Council on American–Islamic Relations (CAIR) in which she said that Muslims have been discriminated against in the US because of 9/11 when 'some people did something', thus tarring all Muslims with the brush of terrorism. Her remarks went unnoticed at the time, despite being broadcast live, but resulted in a video being released by President Donald Trump in April in which images of the Twin Towers falling were superimposed with the words 'some people did something', to imply Omar endorses the 2001 attacks. The key figure in the trajectory of Omar's speech from the CAIR event to the President's thumbs was an Australian 'fake imam', Mohammad Tawhidi, who claimed that she used 9/11 to justify 'the establishment of a terrorist organization (CAIR) on US soil' (Friedersdorf 2019). Death threats against Omar following the release of the video multiplied (Terkel 2019). Despite the fact that the majority of US Democrats failed to speak in support of Omar, right-wing Jewish pundit Ben Shapiro wrote that 'the Democratic Party proved beyond a shadow of a doubt that it is willing to not only countenance but embrace anti-Semitism' (Shapiro 2019). Shapiro's discomfort with antisemitism is selective, it appears, given that he tweeted that, although fellow right-wing commentator Ann Coulter's antisemitic remarks are 'awful, nonsensical', she 'is also super pro-Israel, and has always been so, so I won't lose sleep'.[6]

Antisemitism today, as these vignettes suggest, is not independently identifiable, but relies on an attendant Islamophobia and pro-Zionism that mysteriously slip out of view when it appears on the right and in pro-Israel circles. As the cases of both Orbán and Coulter attest, antisemitism is excused if opposition to Muslims and support for Israel are present. Pro-Zionist politics are not consistent with a rejection of antisemitism, even if the defence of Israel generally presupposes unequivocal support for the Jewish people. Benjamin Netanyahu's self-declaration that, as Prime Minister of Israel, he was the leader of world Jewry cements the inexorable unicity of Jews and Israel such that opposition to left-wing and anti-Zionist Jews is bracketed from 'real antisemitism', which is made synonymous with criticism of Israel. Therefore, Douglas Murray condemns Omar and her supporters for deflecting from her antisemitism by making 'an equivalence between anti-Semitism and the crock term "Islamophobia"' (Murray 2019a). Recalling the definitions of 'real racism' as distinguished from 'not racism' discussed in Chapter 2, Murray describes antisemitism as 'an irrational prejudice built on centuries of stereotypes and hatreds which culminated in the worst crime in human history, on our continent, in the last century'. He contrasts this to Islamophobia, 'a term which can claim almost anything that the wielder claims it to mean' (Murray 2019a), thus endorsing Scruton, who called it 'a propaganda word "invented by the Muslim Brotherhood in order to stop discussion of a major issue"' (Eaton 2019).

The detachment of the definition of antisemitism from that of Islamophobia is bound up with our impoverished public understanding of race. To fully understand the contemporary form taken by race and racial logics requires getting to grips with how, more than any other, debates around the meaning of Islamophobia, and even whether it exists, have been used to discredit the argument that race matters. The proposition that 'Islam is not a race' and that therefore anti-Muslim racism is a misnomer is a core dimension of contemporary Islamophobia. This often relies on a comparison with what is suggested to be the 'real racism' of antisemitism. For example, British journalist David Aaronovitch considers 'that for many perfectly reasonable people a read-across from anti-Semitism to Islamophobia has to be argued, not axiomatically stated. Why? I've explained already. Because Jews are a race/people and Muslims are a faith.'[7] This is a case study in how race attaches itself to and detaches itself from categories and contexts for reasons of political expedience. The multi-ethnic and multinational character of Islam's adherents is considered to disqualify Muslims from being considered 'a race', hence delegitimating the charge that they face racism. In addition to the fact that such a reading erases the existence of Black Jews and Jews of colour, the distinction relies on a purely biologistic account of race that paradoxically reifies it, thus upholding the racialization of the Jews which underpinned the explosion of nineteenth-century political antisemitism. Aaronovitch and others use the argument that Jews are 'a race' while Muslims are 'only' a religion because they seek to negate and downplay Muslim people's experiences of Islamophobia. But this is not as recent a phenomenon as it may seem. Prominent Zionists such as Max Nordau and Arthur Rippin promoted ideas of

'Jewish supremacy', explicitly conceptualized Jews as a race, and presented 'Zionism as a eugenic project' (R. Lentin 2018: 84).

Today's (re-)racialization of Jews flies in the face of Jewish attempts to de-racialize themselves following the Holocaust and to assert themselves instead as a religious minority. Gil Anidjar remarks that Jews in the US refer to themselves as 'American Jews' rather than the reverse in order to press home that 'they would just be a religious minority', rather than an ethnic group for whom being American may be construed as secondary (Shaikh and Anidjar n.d.). The effort to de-racialize oneself is an understandable response to the old European antisemitism that cast Jews as 'a race that was present within all races' (Foucault 2003: 89), a trope that is resurgent on both right and left today, evident in memes that cast Jews as globalist anti-nationalists with dual loyalty to a foreign power. However, the argument is, as Anidjar himself admits, replete with contradictions given that 'Israel both ethnicizes – indeed, racializes – the Jew, and erases the religious difference that is nonetheless critical to its myths and policies' (Shaikh and Anidjar n.d.). This fact was compounded by the 2019 passage of the 'nation state law', which instates 'a racial divide between Jews and Palestinians, and enshrines Jewish supremacy as a core legal principle' (Tatour 2019). It also obscures the fact that in order to become white (Brodkin 1999), non-European Jews had to be re-racialized, thus igniting intra-communal tensions among Jews originating from different parts of the world, with white Jews asserting dominance within the racial landscape of America and Israel predominantly (Slabodsky 2015).

Furthermore, casting doubt on Islamophobia necessitates the mobilization of a 'radical atheist' argument of the sort promoted by Richard Dawkins, in which

Muslims lose legitimacy on the basis of their religiosity. They are cast as *de facto* irrational and opposed to European values, which now incorporate the formerly excluded Jews. In construing Jews as a race in the service of delegitimizing claims of Islamophobia, it is the religion of Islam that is racialized while the religious element of Jewish existence conveniently fades into the background as Judaism is tacitly included within a Eurocentric secularism which also encompasses Christianity. This is clearly evident in the resurfacing of the myth of conjoined 'Judeo-Christianity', which posits, as Ben Shapiro did after the fire that engulfed Notre Dame cathedral in Paris in April 2019, that western civilization was 'built on the Judeo-Christian heritage'.[8] Gene Zubovich locates the origins of 'Judeo-Christianity' in Roosevelt's opposition to rising European antisemitism in the 1930s (Zubovich 2016). However, in its contemporary usage by the right, it is 'an ideological construction' (Burrows 2015) that obscures Christianity's antisemitism and rewrites the history of Europe to exclude Islam and Muslims (Anidjar 2003).

Efforts to counter the Islamophobic manipulation of antisemitism often have recourse to the argument that 'Muslims are the Jews of today'. Discussions about the historical or contemporary possibility of seeing antisemitism and Islamophobia as analogous raise important questions about the specific evolution and purpose of each form of racism (Bunzl 2007). Brian Klug concludes, contra Bunzl's contention that Islamophobia supersedes antisemitism today, that there are sufficient similarities between the two to render the analogy useful (Klug 2014). Arguing about whether antisemitism or Islamophobia is more significant is a pointless exercise given that widely available statistics on the degree of racialized policing, incarceration, everyday discrimination, and violent attacks against Muslims in the West far exceed the number of reported cases of either verbal or physical attacks on Jews. Houria Bouteldja suggests that the attempt to equate Islamophobia and antisemitism is imbricated in a moralist approach to antiracism which, while wishing to recognize the significance of anti-Muslim racism, cannot dispense with the signifier of 'the Jews', 'a community upon which the left progressively re-established its humanist conscience' (Bouteldja 2015). In order to square the circle, progressive leftists create a simple equivalence between anti-Jewish and anti-Muslim racism and elide the fact that institutional and state racism targets Muslims in France but not Jews, although this is not true for all states, Hungary being a case in point. Bouteldja does not deny that antisemitism exists. Rather, her argument is that today, above all, antisemitism describes how 'the Jews', not as people, but as a cipher, serves a purpose for the 'imperialist nation-state' (Bouteldja 2015). As we have seen, this is exacerbated by the readiness of some Jews to excuse antisemitism when doing so serves a larger agenda that includes attacking Muslims, asylum seekers, or, in the US particularly, Black people. Rather than analogous, then, antisemitism and Islamophobia should be thought of as entangled, both historically, in the conjoined purpose of what Anidjar names 'the Jew, the Arab', for defining the external contours of Europe, and contemporarily, as two forms of racism that mutually reinforce each other (Anidjar 2003; Joskowicz 2014; Katz 2018).

Indeed, today, it is no longer useful to theorize antisemitism independently of Islamophobia, although, given that Islamophobia works institutionally as well as chimerically, the inverse is not true. To say that a complete theory of antisemitism requires it to be juxtaposed with the ways in which it is manipulated in the service of anti-Muslim racism is neither to analogize the two nor to dismiss antisemitism as insignificant in its own right. It is to deepen our understanding of why hyper-attention is currently paid to antisemitism. Netanyahu's ahistorical assertion in 2015 that it was the Grand Mufti of Jerusalem who was responsible for the extermination of the Jews of Europe, not Hitler, surely alerts us to the complicity of many Jews with this entangled antisemitism/Islamophobia, sounding warnings about another entanglement, that of Zionism and right-wing Jews with white supremacism (*Haaretz* 2015). The very fact that Islamophobia is so often mobilized in order to draw attention to antisemitism and to contend that Arabs and Muslims should bear the brunt of responsibility for antisemitism should alert us to the role played by racial rule in perpetuating both forms of racism. In other words, while some Jews, as we have seen, are complicit, and antisemitism certainly exists among Muslims, sometimes resulting in violence, neither Jews nor Muslims benefit from the manipulation of antisemitism or the negation of Islamophobia. And antisemitism, while it has been used with great effect over centuries to incite hatred among poorer people in Europe and elsewhere, has always been an elite project, and so it remains.

Weapon or double-edged sword?

A spectre haunts the West, apparently; the spectre of 'Cultural Marxism'. My own entry on the antisemitic Judas Watch website reads, 'Alana Lentin is a Cultural Marxist Jewish Associate Professor'.[9] Those who promote the idea of a 'Cultural Marxist' conspiracy – a linchpin of current right-wing and conservative thought – spread the idea that the mainly Jewish members of the Frankfurt School of social theory and critical philosophy were responsible for using 'psychological manipulation to upend the west'. Cultural Marxism was made into an antisemitic meme by misappropriating the idea of the Frankfurt School thinkers that cultural change is needed to bring about an end to capitalism. Jewish intellectuals who were forced to flee to the US after the rise of Nazism, such as Herbert Marcuse, were targeted for contributing 'to the decline of Western Judeo-Christian civilization' (Garratt 2019). It is not immaterial that Marcuse had taught Black feminist scholar and former political prisoner Angela Davis. Today 'Cultural Marxism' is used to describe 'anti-White traitors, subversives and ... Jewish influence', as the tagline of the Judas Watch website states. It is used to attack 'leftist values' of multiculturalism, 'political correctness', and pro-immigrationism. The story is, as antifascist journalist Jason Wilson puts it, 'transparently barmy' (Wilson 2015). Nonetheless, it has been wildly popular on the right for decades and is rapidly spreading from the fringes of the American conservative movement to the mainstream, as we shall now see.

In a 2019 speech, British Conservative MP Suella Braverman said that she was 'very worried about this ongoing creep of Cultural Marxism which has come from Jeremy Corbyn', a movement she attached to 'politically correct' attacks on free speech at British universities. Cultural Marxism is vague enough a term to see it being co-opted by mainstream politicians, such as Braverman, as a synonym for socialism or poorly defined political correctness. However, this leads to 'its existence in a context of rampant online antisemitism, anti-Muslim sentiment and fervent nationalist populism' being dismissed as inconsequential (Kesvani 2019). The Board of Deputies of British Jews initially rebuked Braverman for using an antisemitic trope. However, after a meeting, they rescinded, stating that 'she is clearly a good friend of the Jewish community', and apologized for any 'distress' caused.[10] Ironically, Braverman found support among opponents of British Labour Party leader Jeremy Corbyn, who had been accused of fostering a culture of antisemitism within the Party. In denial of the fact that the 'Cultural Marxism' trope is used by right-wing actors from Jordan Peterson to Stefan Molyneux in the service of anti-feminism and 'race realism', Braverman's supporters claim that there is nothing antisemitic about the term, given its origins among the Jewish members of the Frankfurt School (Chrenoff 2019). And despite the considerable time spent excoriating those on the left who mobilize 'identity politics', the defence of Braverman centred on her identity as the daughter of Goan immigrants who is married to a Jewish man (Murray 2019b).

The protracted political row over antisemitism in the British Labour Party exemplified the racial logic implicit in thinking about antisemitism as a weapon, rather than as a dimension of racial rule. Defenders of Jeremy Corbyn and other figures in the British Labour movement responded to these claims by stating that, far from being antisemitic, it was their opposition to Israel that their attackers were concerned by. While there is truth in this, the problem with this line of defence is that it denies the possibility of treating antisemitism as separate from debates over Zionism. We must be able to observe antisemitism, even on the left, without always attaching it to a discussion of Israel. In addition, it is a fact that the majority of the world's Jews support the existence of the state of Israel. Yet they do not live there, and many object to the association made on both left and right that, as Donald Trump put it in a Hanukkah address at the White House, Israel is 'their country' (Weisman 2019). Former British Jewish Labour MP Luciana Berger reported receiving hate mail which 'accused me of having two masters. ... They have called me Judas, a Zionazi, and an absolute parasite, and they have told me to get out of this country and go back to Israel' (Burack 2018). The fact that Berger is 'an active supporter of Israel who has visited the country over twenty times' (B. White 2013) is seen as delegitimizing the claim that she faces antisemitism rather than mere objection to her defence of Zionist racism. However, the racism faced by Jewish public figures such as Berger has to be disentangled from her political beliefs, colonialist as they surely are, if antiracism is not to be made contingent on political alignments.

There is a struggle internal to Jewish communities to recognize the pernicious effects of supporting racial-colonial rule through adherence to Israel, abetting antisemitism via shared opposition to Islam and Muslims, and giving succour to white supremacism through support for racist leaders such as Donald Trump and by internally discriminating against Jews of colour (Pierce 2019). The white supremacist attack on the Pittsburgh Tree of Life synagogue in which eleven Jews were murdered in October 2018 shone light on the problematic nature of equating antisemitism exclusively with attacks on white Jews, who, in the post-war era, have been folded into a vision of European identity that excludes people of colour. Addressing a vigil after the mass murder, Black female rabbinical student Tamar Manasseh drew attention to the invisibilization of Black and Brown Jews that occurs as a result of this enfolding, obscuring the fact that Jews were once majority Black and Brown (Gordon 2016; Oxman 2018).

However, the dialogues provoked by these truths are ignored by a culture that has accepted the unilinear story of Jews as white, a reading which serves to render us intelligible to the dominant society (Butler 2006). This need to flatten Jewish experience and complexity, invisibilizing the myriad identity positions and political standpoints within Judaism, participates in the equation of Jews with 'lobbies' or 'forces', as the spread of the 'Cultural Marxist' take-over thesis attests. This is not to say that there are no questions to answer with regard to the impact of Jewish organizations on state policies across the world. However, conflating Jews *tout court* with these processes is, whatever side of the political spectrum one is aligned with, a signal of race at work in terms of the particularity of antisemitism both as a form of racism, and as a mode through which the operations of race are deliberately obscured. Put simply, understanding the complexity of Israeli racial-colonialism, the function of Euro-American Jews vis-à-vis white structures of power, and the impact of the legacy of the Holocaust on the conceptualization of racism will not be served by reducing us to 'the Jews' as a homogeneous identity. What is necessary, rather, is a race-critical reading of what function the equation of all Jews as white and, variably, of all Jews as Zionist has on the operations of racial rule in the current conjuncture. At a fundamental level, the equation of all Jews with Zionism, whether this comes from the pro-Zionist establishment or from those opposed to Israel, is itself a form of antisemitism that refuses the possibility of Jewish divergence from pre-scripted alignments.

The propagation of the idea that the 'Cultural Marxist' agenda is responsible for altering the bases of western civilization is one expression of the widespread idea that the West is subject to manipulation from foreign forces within. There is a point at which legitimate criticism of Israel and of Jewish support for Zionism becomes available to more nefarious pseudo-conspiratorial ideas about the causes of perceived societal dissolution, particularly the perception that a 'traditional working class' and 'dishonoured' white men are losing out at the hands of minorities and migrants, and that there is a politically correct plot in place to bring this about. This can be seen, for example, in the spread of Rothschild memes online claiming that the historical Jewish banking family, as one put it, 'owns every bank in the world ... owns your news, the media, your oil, and your government' (Evon 2016). As a teacher, the ubiquity of these conspiracies was driven home to me when a student used one to make a point about neoliberalism and austerity in a class I teach on 'politics, power and resistance'.

Antisemitism persists memetically despite the successful entry into whiteness of Euro-American Jewish people. This is due to the continued availability of 'the Jews' as a symbol of foreign manipulation, a notion that is core to racist nationalism and was central to the development of intra-European racism in the nineteenth century (Balibar 1991). As Lewis Gordon reminds us, 'Antisemitism is saturated with bad faith [because] most people who hate Jews do not think about their religion. They see the Jews, even if they are white,' as never white enough' (Gordon 2018b: 103). Never being white enough is what undergirds perceived Jewish rootlessness, such that, notwithstanding the dual efforts of Israel and the diaspora Jewish establishment to associate themselves wth hyper-nationalism, 'the Jews' – rather than individual Jewish people – acts as a signifier for an internal threat. This could be seen in the lead-up to the Brexit referendum, which was replete with the manipulation of antisemitic symbols to foment fear about an immigrant take-over that could only be halted by a vote to leave the European Union. A cartoon published on the Leave.eu website used repurposed antisemitic tropes to argue that 'swarthy bearded figures' (now marauding Muslims), carrying bags of money and pushing 'waves of immigration' on a public cowed by the shark of 'political correctness', would be the death knell for 'British culture'. In the popular imagination so successfully captured by this trope, the suffering of the English 'working class', made more acute under austerity, is portrayed as caused by global elites determined to further dispossess them with unwanted migration.

The focus on whether the British Labour Party was held hostage by Zionist forces weaponizing antisemitism to delegitimate the leadership of Jeremy Corbyn has distracted from a more prevalent reality. Some figures within the British labour movement trade on the idea that a far-left, multiculturalist agenda impoverishes and undermines the working class through unfettered support for open borders. The spread in acceptability of this idea unites the anti-immigration right with a nativist left and key figures within the intelligentsia such as the philosopher Slavoj Žižek, who wrote that opening Europe's doors to refugees would 'trigger an instant populist revolt' and result in the triumph of anti-immigrant parties (Žižek 2017).

Katy Brown and her co-authors note that 'populism' has become the go-to word to define 'our current political age', but caution that 'can be a weasel word for "racist"'. They cite the *Guardian*'s observation that whereas about 300 of its articles mentioned populism in 1998, by 2016 2,000 did (K. Brown et al. 2019). The way in which populism is mainly used in these articles and beyond wilfully negates its relation to race and whiteness. Rather, it is construed as prioritizing the 'culture and interests of the nation' and the promise 'to give voice to a people who feel that they have been neglected, even held in contempt, by distant and sometimes corrupt or self-serving elites' (Goodwin 2018). Professor of Politics Matthew Goodwin is one of the key defenders of the thesis that populists are 'not racist'. We met him in Chapter 1 as a *Quillette* magazine contributor and one of the signatories of the letter defending eugenics researcher Noah Carl after his dismissal from Cambridge University. Goodwin claims that the left deliberately misinterprets the positive offer populists make to the electorate, in which curbing immigration is part and parcel of a 'more equal economic settlement' (Goodwin 2018). There is a tacit acceptance in this position that the interests of a cosmopolitan elite are not those of the nation.

In a world in which, the globalization of finance notwithstanding, politics continue to be conducted within nationally bounded territories, the implication that rootless elites foist unwanted migration and multiculturalism onto a disregarded 'indigenous' population only functions if elites themselves are counterfactually portrayed as having extra-national allegiances. Whether or not Jews are named, formulations such as that put forward by Paul Embery (see Introduction) that the divide in society is encapsulated by 'a rootless, cosmopolitan, bohemian middle-class ... and a rooted, communitarian, patriotic working-class'[11] function chimerically to evoke the spectre of a core European Manicheanism. As political sociologist David Smith puts it, 'These ghostly, walking tropes are not Jews. They are representations of people, not people per se' (D. Smith 1996: 221). Hence, they represent a grab bag into which can be thrown everything that challenges what is presented as the originary legitimate right of white people to the fruits of the nation. The point is not whether individual Jews are responsible for particular acts. Smith agrees that 'antisemites take the actual Jews of history as their premise' (D. Smith 1996: 221). However, he resists the implication of Hannah Arendt's thesis that some Jewish financiers were responsible for detrimentally affecting society, despite becoming 'the victim of the world's injustice and cruelty' (Arendt 1951: 8). Jewish actions may 'inspire chimerical fantasy', but Jews cannot be held co-responsible for antisemitism (D. Smith 1996: 221). To take Arendt's side would be to agree that the fact that some migrants are criminals or that some Muslims have perpetrated acts of terrorism means that, *qua* migrants or Muslims, they can be held responsible for racism. It is far from new to argue that stopping immigration is a panacea for racism, as witnessed in the refusal of both Australia and Ireland to allow Jewish refugees fleeing Nazism entry into their countries in the 1930s. Both countries argued that allowing Jews in would lead to an increase in racism. Indeed, a core rationale of popular anti-immigrationism is that it is reasonable to demand that immigrants integrate into 'our way of life' or face sanction, and that the failure to do so – not a discriminatory and carceral migration regime – is what conjures an otherwise dormant racism.

Separating Jewish actions from antisemitic interpretations, far from absolving individual Jews, the representatives of certain Jewish institutions, or Zionist colonial ideology of responsibility for damaging actions, frees us to identify them without attaching them racistly to an underlying, homogenizing 'genetic code' (S. Hall 2017). Seen in this way, it was not antisemitic for Ilhan Omar to accuse Stephen Miller, the architect of Donald Trump's migration policies, which include the travel ban on people from Muslim countries and the policy of separating children from their families at the Southern border, of being a white nationalist. Miller has said he 'would be happy if not a single refugee foot ever again touched American soil' (Levitz 2019), encouraging his uncle to evoke the family history of escape from Nazi Europe and ask his nephew in an open letter 'if the chanting, torch-bearing Nazis of Charlottesville, whose support his boss seems to court so cavalierly, do not envision a similar fate for him' (Glosser 2018). However, this should not be taken to mean that antisemitism is wholly fictitious, a reading that would lend itself to the adjudication of all racisms on a case-by-case basis that disables the analysis on which this book is based: that race is above all a matter of rule. What the simplification of debates over antisem-itism neglect in their pitting of weaponization against ubiquitous Jew hatred is an interpretation of the place accorded to the 'frozen racism' of modern antisemitism in the overall architecture of race.

Decolonizing antisemitism

On 16 February 2019, French 'new philosopher' and public provocateur Alain Finkielkraut was verbally abused by protesters aligned with the *Gilets jaunes* grass-roots movement for economic justice that had exploded onto the scene late the previous year. They called him a 'dirty Zionist' and told him to 'go back to Tel Aviv'.

The protesters were identified as pro-Palestinian, or, to use the expression of the Islamophobic *Riposte laïque* website, 'pro-Palestinian, lefties, fascists and Muslims' (Moisan 2019). This was hegemonically interpreted as an antisemitic attack. In its aftermath, President Emmanuel Macron called anti-Zionism a form of antisemitism such as not seen 'since the Second World War' (Bouteldja and Lentin 2019).[12]

Finkielkraut is a central figure in French Islamophobia and an outspoken defender of Zionism. *Riposte laïque* came to his defence notwithstanding their rejection of his anti-Trump standpoints or of his opposition to the antisemitism of the comedian Dieudonné. For these 'right and left wing patriots' and defenders of the Republic who refuse to 'accept the Islamization of their country',[13] those who attacked Finkielkraut were 'degenerate, hateful' imposters who do not have the '*Gilets jaunes* culture' within them (Moisan 2019). Yet Finkielkraut himself maintained, in November 2018, that the yellow-vested protesters, as the 'left behind of happy globalization', have every right to voice their opposition to 'progressivist thinking ... characterized by the refusal to take into account the economic and cultural insecurity of the middle and working classes', hence mobilizing an anti-globalist argument of the kind that pits the 'rootless' against the 'rooted' (Feertchak 2018). It is interesting that Finkielkraut chose to reference globalization in this way, given the antisemitic undertones of the terms 'globalism' or 'globalist' (Barenblat 2018). Trump has called himself a 'nationalist' in comparison to a 'globalist', who is 'a person that wants the globe to do well, frankly, not caring about our country so much' (Boyer 2018). The Australian Prime Minister, Scott Morrison, has spoken about a 'negative globalism' run by an 'unaccountable internationalist bureaucracy' (Karp 2019). Be that as it may, as soon as Finkielkraut became the object of 'pro-Palestinian' abuse, his position on the *Gilets jaunes* changed from one which saw them as the patriotic little people forgotten by globalist elites to one which regarded them as the embodiment of antisemitism. He expresses the commonly held view in France that antiracism has become the object of a 'terrible corruption' by Islamic-leftists and communitarians (Nadau 2019). This view plays a not insignificant role in the rise of violent Islamophobia and antiblackness in France today.

A few days after the attack on Finkielkraut, a rally against antisemitism was held in the centre of Paris, attended by the French government, all the major political parties, the official representatives of the French Jewish communities, and major antiracism organizations. This curious gathering, which recalled the march attended by world leaders, including Benjamin Netanyahu, after the 2015 *Charlie Hebdo* attacks, signified a state-endorsed, top-down antiracism which is at odds with the grassroots mobilization of racialized people, including many Jews.

There is no reason to assume that the *Gilets jaunes* would be any less infused with antisemitic symbols than any other political movement at a time when memetic antisemitism has, as I have noted, become widely available across the political spectrum (Assoun 2019). The existence of antisemitic tropes within the *Gilets jaunes* movement notwithstanding, including the circulation of memes attaching President Emmanuel Macron to the 'Rothschilds' (Hirsch 2019), it is vital to set the labelling of the movement as uniquely antisemitic in the context of a French state, and, more generally, of a West, coming face-to-face with the ramifications of a 'dying colonialism' (Fanon 2007

[1965]). Post-Holocaust European states in their declaration that 'never again' would genocide take place on European soil operated with a cognitively dissonant denial of the fact that colonization had not stopped. Europe was still exploiting and racially dominating its colonized and formerly colonized 'others' both in the majority world and within the frontiers of the rapidly diversifying metropoles of the post-war years.

In effect, then, concern for antisemitism, which is morally defined as aberrant and ignorant, is transposed onto racism in general. This produces a vague humanist and universalizing form of antiracism which enjoys state support and that, because of this, downplays institutionalized or state racism (Bouteldja 2015). To situate racism in the instruments of state rule, rather than in the bad faith of individuals or in particular, uniquely antisemitic communities – primarily Muslims – would mean admitting that the rejection of race that united the European states after the Holocaust had a specific purpose: to cleanse Europe of its Judeophobia without dislodging racial-colonial governance abroad or the exploitation of non-European migrants at home.

Not only is antisemitism a chimera, then, but the fight against it increasingly takes on a chimeric form. As David Smith puts it, 'Chimerical antisemitism often rises to obsessional as well as delusional heights' (D. Smith 1996: 222). So, too, official, top-down antiracism relies on a mirror of this delusion and sets antisemitism up as the threat to end all threats. This does not, as we have seen, result in an end to antisemitism. Rather, antisemitism is left intact while all other racisms within the racial state are denied. A two-sided vision has solidified in which either antisemitism is the fruit of an uncritical left-wing Islamophilia that creates what in France has become known as '*Islamogauchisme*' (Islamic leftism),

Official, top-down antiracism sets antisemitism up as the threat to end all threats with the purpose not of ending antisemitism, but of denying all other racisms within the racial state.

or it is purely a tool to undermine the pro-Palestine movement. Complexifying this polarity are the voices of race-critical, anticolonial Jews and our allies. However, the activism and scholarship that produce a decolonial reading of antisemitism, drawing out its imbrication in other forms of racial rule and its availability as a narrative to racial states, are either ignored or savagely misrepresented in the public arena, as the attacks on anti-Zionist Jews attest.

To fully understand the political utility of antisemitism and the possibility, as I have shown, for particular antisemitic tropes, such as globalism, rootlessness, and 'Cultural Marxism', to coexist with a performative defence of Jews and Israel against an antisemitism made synonymous with anti-Zionism, we need to take a close look at the role played by 'state philosemitism' (Bouteldja 2015). Exposing the role played by philosemitic alignments today is key to the process of decolonizing antisemitism and revealing how race plays a crucial role in building hierarchies of victimhood with pernicious effects. The false love for Jews relies on the separation of 'good' from 'bad' Jews, as I later elaborate (see also Topolski 2018). Only the good Jews are its beneficiaries. To receive philosemitic love, Jews in France must uphold the dominant French narrative of Islamophobia which the sociologist Ugo Palheta, author of *The Possibility of Fascism*, has called a 'new nationalist and racist doxa'. Being a 'bad Jew' means to align with Muslims, 'the enemy within' (Palheta 2019) – a role once ascribed to the Jews.

State philosemitism does not denote actual love of Jews or concern with antisemitism against all Jews. If that were the case, the antisemitism waged against anti-Zionist Jews, Black Jews, Jews of colour, and

164

all those who do not fit into a template of what the modern Jewish subject of the post-Holocaust looks like would be equally protected from charges of traitorship and 'self-hatred'. The philosemitic defence of Jews and Israel relies on the tacit acceptance of the idea of Jews as perennial foreigners. Houria Bouteldja states that even while Jews are being defended, French citizens and Jews are always talked about as separate in official French discourse. This reveals how '"Jews" as a category are still not a fully legitimate part of the nation and its identity' (Bouteldja 2015). This was evident in President Raymond Barre's condemnation of the 1980 attack on a synagogue which 'intended to strike Israelites who were going to the synagogue and which struck innocent French people who were crossing the rue Copernic' (Assoun 2019). Similarly, in 2004, Jacques Chirac noted the rise in racist attacks against 'our Jewish or Muslim compatriots, or sometimes quite simply against the French' (Bouteldja 2015).

State philosemitism emerges as a function of Europe's realization that it had applied colonialist procedures on its own soil against white people and, as Aimé Césaire put it, no longer 'merely' against 'the Arabs of Algeria, the "coolies" of India, or the "niggers" of Africa' (Césaire 2000 [1955]: 36). Rudolf Bkouche notes that it was the Holocaust that made white people out of Jews, reminding us of Catholic monarchist Georges Bernanos's 'terrible words' that 'after the massacre it was no longer possible to be antisemitic', as though, if it were not for the Holocaust, antisemitism could have continued as usual (Bkouche 2015).

State philosemitism, thus, takes independent agency away from Jews and 'unilaterally squeezes us between the forces of power and the popular masses' (Assoun 2019). This positioning is what permits Jews in France to become what Bouteldja has referred to as the '*dhimmis* of the Republic', the *dhimmis* being those Jews and Christians who were accorded protected status under Arab rule in the past (Bouteldja 2016: 51). Positioned such, Jews become aligned with the needs of the state and whiteness. For this polemic and others, Bouteldja has been accused of antisemitism. Her 2016 book *Whites, Jews and Us* was widely attacked in France, with the attacks often based on wilful misreadings. For example, in the chapter addressed to Jews, Bouteldja mentions that a cousin from back home in Algeria does not know who Hitler is. She shocked readers by writing that this cousin's words are precious. But they are precious because they remind us that at its core 'antisemitism is European'. It does not derive from Muslims or the Arab world. If it exists there today, it has been bequeathed by colonialism (Bouteldja 2016: 55). Nonetheless, attacks on Bouteldja multiply even as her book gains readers and scholarly support across the world (Fernando and Lloyd 2018). One of her detractors, the political scientist Thomas Guénolé, is a member of the main left party of opposition in France, *La France insoumise*. He accuses her of racism and antisemitism (A. Lentin and signatories 2017). In so doing, Guénolé ignores the subheading of the book, 'a politics of revolutionary love', for *Whites, Jews and Us* is a lament for the lost past in common of Jews and Muslims in the Arab world.

Simon Assoun, an anti-Zionist member of the French Union of Jews for Peace and a *Gilet jaune*, agrees with Bouteldja that there is a pernicious state philosemitism in France. Being made the '*dhimmis* of the Republic' has no benefit for Jewish people. On the contrary, it equates 'the Jews' with power, leaving them open to antisemitic attack (Assoun 2019).

Assoun contends that when the French government and 'its *dhimmis*' held the aforementioned protest against antisemitism that followed the attack by some *Gilets jaunes* on Alain Finkielkraut, it served to take the spotlight off rising popular protest. These protests against the Macron government's neoliberal policies were discredited by associating participants with antisemitism. Far from being effective to combat real antisemitism, which Assoun does not deny exists on both the right and the left, this only served to demonize Jewish people. Furthermore, by constructing a figure of the 'innocent Jew' (Assoun 2019), the complexity of Jewish existence is flattened. It renders invisible the history of Jewish trade unionism and anticolonialism, the role of South African Jews in the anti-Apartheid movement and the Israeli Black Panther movement, the movement of Black Jews against racism and the Israeli movement against anti-immigrant racism, as well as Jewish involvement in the struggle for a free Palestine invisible.

In *The Crises of Multiculturalism*, Gavan Titley and I argued that the state mobilizes two visions of diversity – good and bad. Good diversity foregrounds the 'neoliberal formation of the autonomous, self-sufficient subject': the model migrant, for example (A. Lentin and Titley 2011: 6). She is pitted against the subject of 'bad diversity', who embodies an excess of culture of the wrong kind and places strain on resources nationalistically construed as finite. In today's Islamophobic times, the subjects of 'bad diversity' are most often religious and politically engaged Muslims. Analogously, philosemitism constructs good and bad Jews. This Manichean view hides the fact that support for Jews is always conditional on performing the role expected from us by the state and public sphere eager to distance themselves from the racism of today. 'Real racism' must remain firmly in the past. In this scenario there are also 'good' Muslims and 'bad' Muslims, reminding us why both Jews and Muslims are served by solidarity not enmity. 'Good Muslims' cooperate with the state in the war on terror; 'bad Muslims' resist it (Morsi 2017). Not only are there two types of Jews and two types of Muslims, but there are two types of antisemitism. Bad antisemitism is 'real'; it exists among the far-right, the far-left, and Muslims. In contrast, 'good antisemitism', which treats Jews as a racialized subaltern group in service to the state, is left intact.

Bad Jews are those who refuse to allow antisemitism to be instrumentalized in the service of racial rule. They are anti-Zionist and struggle against racism in all its forms (Bouteldja and Lentin 2019). The bad Jew who refuses to sit in her accorded place is the thorn in the side of the racial state. The argument I have made here, that antisemitism cannot be disentangled from other forms of racism – most prominently Islamophobia, but also antiblackness, anti-Roma racism, and anti-migrant racism which builds on earlier forms that explicitly targeted Jews as unwanted aliens – should not be taken to mean that antisemitism no longer exists. Rather, a decolonial and race-critical reading of antisemitism requires it to be considered against the question of where anti-Jewish racism sits in the archipelago of racial rule. Nevertheless, I wish to note the specific forms taken by antisemitism – its cipherization, its availability to racial rule and the proxification of antiracism, and the attendant construction of good and bad Jews – in order to better act against it.

After the Holocaust, making race into a taboo did nothing to assist a deeper understanding of the history and political sociology of modern racial rule or help counter racism (A. Lentin 2008). Similarly today, considering a unidimensional account of 'bad antisemitism' as the prototype for all racisms rather than setting it in the context of colonial modernity and its continued imprint will do little for the fight against antisemitism. From my perspective as a Jew, I agree with Santiago Slabodsky that this approach also pushes Jews further adrift from what he calls our barbarian history, the history which ties us to the other subjects of racial rule (Slabodsky 2015). Slabodsky, contra the hegemonic Zionist preference for a Jew to 'be a Maccabee – not a Hellenized dweeb',[14] wishes for us to dwell in the realm of Jewish suffering. This is not in order to elevate our persecution above that of others, as hegemonic readings of the Holocaust would have it, but in order to draw a line from our experience to that of others, drawing attention to commonalities in the ways we have suffered. To recall the discussion of victimhood and trauma in Chapter 3, taking this approach does not require that we reassert victimhood perennially, but that we draw on our past, not only to build solidarity decolonially, but also to unveil the ways in which racial rule necessarily shapeshifts, never remaining the same.

However, as Slabodsky concludes, there are no guarantees as to the outcome of this sitting with suffering. Suffering, as we have seen, is available politically both to hegemonic projects and to subversive ones. Today, it is no longer possible to simply repeat Fanon's reminder that 'an anti-Semite is inevitably anti-Negro' (Fanon 1986 [1967]: 122), or that of bell hooks that 'white supremacy relies on the maintenance of anti-black racism and antisemitism' (hooks 1995: 213). Just as it is insufficient to remark that race is a social construct, we need to work hard to unveil *how* this is so; how antisemitism, antiblackness, Islamophobia, coloniality, and white supremacy work co-constitutively. This is, as Stuart Hall put it, a 'politics without guarantees', as I shall now propose in conclusion.

Conclusion: Talking and Not Talking about Race

This book has surely raised more questions than it has provided answers. However, the difference between those who question race and those who merely accept it is the difference between the 'race realist' and the race-critical antiracist. 'Race realists' are racists; race critics fight racism. We use the tools at our disposal to expose how race is produced and reproduced; how it attaches to a range of political, economic, familial, sexual, and social projects; how it coalesces with gender and hetero-sexualism; and how it is deeply tied to the past and present of capitalism and to the structures of knowledge production.

Between these two groups – racist and race-critical antiracist – there are those who choose to be silent about race. They believe that the best way to challenge racism is to refuse to speak about race. They fear that referring to race risks naturalizing and solidifying human distinctions. But it is not race-critical scholarship or activism that creates racists. Racists are created by the conditions established by racial rule over the course of modernity. So, as I hope to have convinced you, it is not by refusing to make reference to race that it will matter less. Race matters regardless of these good intentions. We are not served by talking in euphemisms or pretending that race belongs to the past.

In May 2018, hundreds of people, almost all Black and Brown, gathered in the town hall at Saint Denis, a working-class neighbourhood of Paris, for the 'Bandung of the Global North' conference, recalling the 1955 'intercontinental gathering of people of colour' held in Bandung, Indonesia ('Bandung du Nord' 2018). The hall, which had seen better days, was abuzz. Angela Davis was headlining the opening night. The participants stayed for an entire weekend. They listened, they contested, they cheered, and they danced.

I met David Palumbo-Liu there. David is a staunch activist for Palestine and against fascism on US campuses. He writes that the 'Bandung conference' took place on the fiftieth anniversary of May 1968, and cites the sociologist Nacira Guénif-Souilamas, who said that the 2018 event was

> a way to distance ourselves from the narrative of 1968, as it was told in the mainstream media by the French elite, who feel that 1968 belongs to them. Things are happening now that require another narrative of what '68 was. We [indigenous people of colour] do not belong to the north – we happen to be in the north. Therefore, we have a vantage point to understand the north in a particularly critical way. (Palumbo-Liu 2018)

Guénif-Souilamas's words recall those of Ambalavaner Sivanandan, who reminded the British that 'we are here because you were there' (Younge 2018).

Across town at the same time as the Bandung conference was taking place, an anti-austerity demonstration was organized by *La France insoumise*. As

Conclusion: Talking and Not Talking about Race

Houria Bouteldja, one of the Bandung conference organizers, noted in her address, 'This demonstration, which I welcome personally as I welcome the strikes that are going on right now ... is almost an allegory of our spaces, our times, of our parallel worlds: white and *indigènes*.[1] Them in Paris, us in Saint Denis.' Race and class came together at the Bandung conference. Race should have mattered to the anti-austerity protesters too. As Stuart Hall noted almost forty years previously, observing debates within the labour movement in Britain, 'The structures through which black labour is reproduced ... are not simply "coloured" by race; they work through race. ... Race ... is the modality through which class is lived' (S. Hall 1980: 340). Black and other racialized people, activists and scholars have not had the privilege of ignoring how race matters. They have been explaining it in many different ways and in many different spaces. Yet those for whom it is more comforting to believe that race does not matter, or that it matters less than it used to, or less than other forms of oppression, often do not listen.

No one finds it easy to admit that they benefit from racial arrangements, as Robin DiAngelo shows in her book on 'white fragility' (DiAngelo 2018). In Chapter 2, my discussion of the dominance of the narrative of 'not racism' revealed that, because many white people have come to conflate talking about race with being personally accused of racism, race as a matter of serious study and discussion is avoided. My argument is that pretending race does not matter does not make it go away. Instead it lingers and festers. I do not argue that race *should* matter, but that it simply *does* matter, today, but hopefully not forever.

One of the reasons why it has been so easy to claim that race does not matter is because Black, Indigenous, and

173

other racialized people, who have first-hand experience of racism, are still not heard from often enough in the public sphere. Their scholarship is marginalized, and they face institutional racism. Consequently, as I have argued, the public is not equipped with the racial literacy needed to make sense of the historical conditions that made race matter. When people who face racism do speak about race, they are often heard as needlessly complaining. We can witness the inequities established in the name of race when racialized people are silenced. When they do speak, white publics are forced to address the fact that this is all too rare, and that much of what people of colour say about race is heard through the filter of epistemic Eurocentrism, in which we have been steeped from a young age. Thanks to racial-colonial rule, this is not even confined to the Global North. The Kenyan author Ngũgĩ wa Thiong'o wrote of the ubiquity of English-language education in Africa that: 'The language of power is English and that becomes internalized. ... You normalize the abnormal and the absurdities of colonialism, and turn them into a norm from which you operate. Then you don't even think about it' (Wade 2018).

Reproducing racial-colonial knowledge is an ongoing endeavour. For example, the Australian government has spent $48.7 million to mark the 250th anniversary of Captain James Cook's first voyage to Australia and the Pacific in 1768. The primary school curriculum is replete with narrations of the endeavours of the 'First Fleet'. The simple request not to celebrate Australia Day on the day Aboriginal lands were invaded is met with white protesters carrying banners reading 'To defend my country was once called patriotism, now it's called racism' (Loomes and Bedo 2019).

Choosing not to make race matter, then, is inextricably tied to assumptions about who can be a knower

(Collins 2000; L. T. Smith 2012). It is driven by what Gurminder Bhambra calls 'methodological whiteness' which distorts 'social scientific accounts' (Bhambra 2017: S214). There are many things that are known about racialized people, knowledge that is used in their continued subjugation, the data collected expanding infinitely in our hyper-surveilled, digitized, always-on landscape, where, for many, the street, not the prison, has become the panopticon (Browne 2015; Vitale and Jefferson 2016). But knowledge elaborated by Black, Brown, Indigenous, Muslim, Roma, and other racialized people, particularly knowledge about race, is regarded as suspect. It is common to hear it said that to understand race and racism requires objectivity, and that only unaffected bystanders have the capacity for interpretation. Being too close to the experience of racism, it is suggested, leads to emotion taking over from reason (Zuberi and Bonilla-Silva 2008). This unfounded belief at the heart of an epistemically racist positivism contributes to the idea that race does not really matter and that making it matter too much is the thorn in the side of a happier future. This is born of the white ignorance that is not actual ignorance but the false ignorance of those who wish to dictate what is knowable (Grosfoguel 2015; Mills 2007). It speaks in the tones of white innocence, of we did not know, we were not told (Wekker 2016). The public is able to tell itself that race does not matter because the West has sidelined Indigenous and Black perspectives and treated the knowledges of the majority of the world as inferior.

This is illustrated by Aboriginal (Munanjahli) and South Sea Islander scholar Chelsea Bond's contribution to a 2019 event held at Melbourne's La Trobe University titled 'Has Racism in Contemporary Australia Entered the Political Mainstream?' The event was originally pitched as a debate between the former Race Discrimination Commissioner and the director of a conservative think-tank, and had the title 'Does Australia Still Have a Serious Racism Problem?' This was changed after an open letter challenging it was signed by 170 people. The failure to include the perspectives of Aboriginal or other racialized women led to Bond being invited to speak. She unrelentingly reminded the audience that, despite Aboriginal people's expertise on matters of race, her inclusion was an afterthought and her placement last on the line-up of speakers revealed how little respect is given to Black scholarship in Australia.

Allen Elbourne, a husband, father, and Pacific Islander migrant activist, told me that Bond's words reminded him of those of African-American lesbian poet Audre Lorde, who, incongruously, we agreed, had been invited to address a women's writing conference held in 1985 to mark the 150th anniversary of the foundation of Victoria, 'an Australian State built upon racism, destruction, and a borrowed sameness' (Lorde 2017: 63). Both Bond and Lorde refused to be manipulated for the whitewashing of racial-colonial history. 'Australian history has more than a racial dimension,' Bond said. 'Race has been foundational to this country, it arrived on the ships in 1788,' she continued, thus instantly undoing the thinking that made it possible to consider racism a matter for debate (La Trobe University 2019).

Lorde, in her address, expressed puzzlement as to why she had been brought to address the sea of white women before her when her sister Aboriginal and Torres Strait Islander women had been left out. She recalled the 'terrible amount of Wurundjeri women's blood [that] has already been shed in order for you to sit and write here' (Lorde 2017: 65). She told her audience that 'it would be an error to believe that we mean the same experience, the same commitment, the same future, unless we agree to examine the history and the particular passions that lie beneath each other's words' (Lorde 2017: 64). Neither Lorde nor Bond accepted that history can be put aside even in the laudable aim of finding common ground, and neither guilt nor romanticism, as Lorde put it, would be of any use to that end. Both were clearly stating facts, not appealing to white benevolence. I heard them both echoed in Frantz Fanon, who in his collection of previously unpublished writings, *Alienation and Freedom* remarked,

> If we can point to a sterile approach, then it is one that consists, for an oppressed person, in trying to speak to the 'heart' of his oppressors: history contains no example of a dominant power yielding to the tongue-lashings, however reasonable and moving, of those that it crushes; against material interests, sentiments and good sense are never heard. (Fanon 2018: 637)

The obstinance of white denial and 'not racism' reveals this unbendable truth. Fanon, Lorde, and Bond lay bare the futility of meeting each act of violence, every narrative of 'great replacement', of cultural incompatibility, ethnicized extremism, dual loyalty, insidious influence, genetic propensity, resource finiteness, or white anxiety with an appeal for more band-aids in the form of diversity fests, inquests, and promises to do better. There is no will to know, there is only the will to defend and obfuscate.

'This is a war for control, this is a war for the little guy,' says white ideologue Steve Bannon.[2] As we have seen, too many social and political scientists, psychologists, journalists, and mainstream politicians choose to respond to this declaration of violence with an appeal for compassion for discomfited white people. They present this as a non-racial response, as a way of de-escalating what they interpret as 'complex race relations', as though there were two equal parts at play with right and wrong on 'both sides', as Donald Trump put it after white supremacists marched on Charlottesville. This textbook example of 'white innocence' is steeped in the racial logic it will not admit. It equates to choosing whiteness, the very category race was installed to establish, defend, and maintain. Nonetheless, the pretence that none of this is about race is most disturbingly portrayed as being better for everyone, including those racialized as other than white.

In conclusion, let us imagine that a time has been reached when race and the discourses and forms of governance created in its name are a thing of the past, when structural white advantage has been dismantled, and when racist discrimination and violence no longer occur. At such a time, we might hear stories about the meanings of race and of how it was addressed, fought against, and overcome. An interesting story might unfurl. In this story, studying the history of race and discussing its effects would not equate to simplifying more complex processes, as many think it does today. It would mean opening a door to a history that, although crucial to the formation of the modern world system, has largely been treated as a special interest topic, or a drum endlessly beaten by those who just won't move on.

Unfortunately, however, if we are attentive to how it works, we need race as a tool of analysis to interpret other structures of power – capitalism, gender, sexuality, class, and ability – as fully as possible also. The simple question remains: how can we dismantle race without studying it? We need to strip back the façade and reveal

Ignoring race and
denying that it
matters or reaching
for euphemisms that
comfort white anxieties
will not make race
matter any less than it
does.

the building blocks of the 'master's house' in order to understand how it was built. I therefore insist that being critically attentive to race is political. It is possible to use race as an analytical tool without regressing to the separatist margins, as many on the left would have it. This is not easy, and it is much easier not to do so. But we cannot do away with race yet. We cannot get to an end point before running a course whose finish line is still out of sight.

Note, however, that this is not a pessimistic ending. The critical conversations that need to happen about race are happening. Blacks and Arabs, Muslims and Jews, First Nations and African-American people, Aboriginal and Muslim people, any other cross-cut of this and everyone with refugees. We are talking, and white people committed to the dismantling of racial advantage are participating too. The talk can often be fraught with the tensions produced by a racial-colonial system which hierarchizes and divides. However, it is here that the difficult things are being said. This is a politics that Stuart Hall would have described as having no guarantees (S. Hall 2017). There are no sureties, no strategies to follow that will ensure a desired outcome. What can be guaranteed is that ignoring race and denying that it matters or reaching for euphemisms that comfort white anxieties will not make race matter any less than it does. Race still matters and this is not acceptable. Objections alone will not make race matter any less. What does matter is what we are doing to make it not matter in the future.

Notes

Chapter 1 Race beyond Social Construction

1 I would like to thank Fleur Ramsay for drawing my attention to this incident.

2 I argued this point in an open letter written on behalf of the Australian Critical Race & Whiteness Studies Association to the editors of the *Monash Bioethics Review* (Media Diversified 2018).

3 For example, the practices of forced sterilization are still in use against Indigenous women in Canada (Kirkup 2018).

4 *https://cehg.stanford.edu/letter-from-population-geneticists*.

5 In her book *The Biopolitics of Feeling*, Kyla Schuller exposes the fact that despite this, Du Bois also aimed to 'improve the racial stock' by promoting 'family planning measures such as birth control and adoption as tools for the biocultural transformation of the black working class' (Schuller 2017: 175).

6 Statement by Professor Kim TallBear. *https://twitter.com/kimtallbear/status/1051906470923493377?lang=en*.

7 Tweet by Claire Lehmann, 29 July 2019. *https://twitter.com/clairlemon/status/1155597002530365442*.

8 For example, the American Civil Liberties Union reported in December 2018 that Amazon has made a patent application to develop a doorbell that would use face surveillance to alert police to people whom residents find suspicious. The device would allow residents to add photos of 'suspicious' people from a database which the doorbell's facial recognition software would scan when people pass by their door. This technology is disturbing given reports that white residents in the US have threatened Black people who have come to their door, such as in the widely reported case of a Black teenager who approached a house after he missed his school bus and was shot at by the occupier (Kekatos 2018).

9 *https://www.diabetesaustralia.com.au/ aboriginal-and-torres-strait-islanders.*

10 Tweet by Eric Kaufmann, 1 May 2019. *https://twitter. com/epkaufm/status/1123482483998298113.*

Chapter 2 'Not Racism™'

1 Tweet by Yashar Ali, 16 January 2019. *https://twitter. com/yashar/status/1085228801003540485.*

2 Tweet by Donald Trump, 16 July 2019. *https://twitter. com/realdonaldtrump/status/1151129281134768128?la ng=en.*

3 The AGRIF (General Alliance Against Racism and for the Respect of French and Christian Identity) is described as 'one of the satellites in the constellation of the Catholic and traditionalist, ultranationalist and racist Right; an influential widespread current which converges with notorious anti-Semitic former collaborators of the Vichy regime, fervent supporters of colonization, former members and sympathizers of the terrorist group of ultraright bent OAS (from the French, *Organisation de l'Armée Secrète*), Christian fundamentalists, and others nostalgic for the Crusades.' 'Party of the Indigenous of

the Republic Threatened in France', 8 June 2010. *http:// readersupportednews.org/pm-section/21-21/2149-party- of-the-indigenous-of-the-republic-threatened-in-france.*

4 For another account of Kaufmann's notion of 'racial self- interest', see Bhambra (2017).

5 David Goodhart wrote in a 2004 *Prospect* magazine article that 'if values become more diverse, if lifestyles become more differentiated, then it becomes more difficult to sustain the legitimacy of a universal risk-pooling welfare state' (Goodhart 2004). Since then, Goodhart, described as a 'liberal Powellite' by former head of the British Commission for Racial Equality Trevor Phillips (himself one of the key voices in decrying the failures of multicul- turalism), has moved steadily to the right (A. Lentin and Titley 2011). His 2017 book *The Road to Somewhere* (Goodhart 2017a) presents a vision of British society split between rooted 'somewhere' people and footloose 'anywhere' people. It is an echo of Theresa May's claim when UK Prime Minister that 'if you believe you are a citizen of the world, you are a citizen of nowhere' (May 2016).

6 Tweet by Richard Dawkins, 25 July 2017. *https://twitter. com/richarddawkins/status/889819353906110474?la ng=en.*

Chapter 3 Making It about Race

1 This was the view expressed in a tweet by popular antiracist account David Lo Pun-ch Nazis, 5 September 2018. *https://twitter.com/helpmeskeletor/status/1037152 660103749632.* And Aboriginal playwright and actor, Nakkiah Lui tweeted on 5 September 2018, 'That's the problem with the Left. It's like the Right but the whiteness is subversive. It doesn't want to change or dismantle values of power, it just wants to make it look different. Tonightly should call their video Bootcamp for white

lefties ... or maybe just learn to listen.' *https://twitter.com/ nakkiahlui/status/1037376797292281857.*

2 Intelligence Squared debate, 'Should Australia Curb Immigration?', 26 March 2019. *https://ethics.org.au/ experience/iq2-debate-curb-immigration/.*

3 Tweet by Lisa Mckenzie archived by the author on 17 September 2015.

4 Tweet by Libcom, 22 March 2019. *https://twitter.com/ libcomorg/status/1109066183251279872.*

5 Streeck repeats the talking points of the anti-immigrant right when he falsely claims that refugees and asylum seekers in Germany receive entitlements that 'are often much higher, making them feel abandoned by their government in favor of strangers' (Streeck 2017). This instantly raised alarm bells for me, so I contacted the German NGO *ProAsyl*, which campaigns for asylum seekers' rights, as well as two German-based colleagues, Stefanie Boulila and Cristiane Carri, who pointed me to the relevant tables published by the *Bundesministerium der Justiz und für Verbraucherschutz*, which reveal that a single German welfare claimant receives almost four times more per month than an asylum seeker. Kira Pieper has also analysed the popular right-wing mythical talking point that asylum seekers receive more welfare payments than Germans (Piper 2016), demonstrating that Streeck is content to parrot these unempirical arguments rather than engage in basic research.

6 'Since World War II, the German Muselmann has referred specifically to the death camps and, although the derivation of the term within the camps is clouded by uncertainty, no one has been able to explain – not for lack of specu-lation – why it was this term and not another that came to be associated with this condition. Agamben believes it to reference the Arabic signification of Muslim, "the one who submits unconditionally to the will of Allah."

However, this theological explanation does not appear in the testimonies collected by Polish sociologists Zdzislaw Ryn and Stanslav Klodzinski. In these testimonies, former inmates frequently mention Muselmänner wearing scarves around their heads or wrapping blankets around their bodies to keep warm as a likely explanation of the term's widespread utilization across different languages (besides German, similar Polish and French words were also used) in the camps. Most scholars who write about the Muselmann do not pause to reflect on the name of this figure, thereby leaving intact the bonding of an abject process/status to a racio-religious label' (Weheliye 2014: 54).

7 Frank Wilderson has claimed that Arab antiblackness meant that the experiences of Black people in Ferguson and those of Palestinians under occupation were incomparable (Ball 2014).

Chapter 4 Good Jew/Bad Jew

1 *http://img1.vnnforum.com/showthread.php?t=157785.*

2 Tweet by Jacob Rees-Mogg, 14 April 2019. *https://twitter.com/Jacob_Rees_Mogg/status/1117471965235810304.*

3 *https://www.youtube.com/watch?v=8dNjsSWxCKM.* Boris Johnson would become Prime Minister three months later.

4 Tweet by Stephen Pollard, 10 April 2019. *https://twitter.com/stephenpollard/status/1116056603218841600.*

5 Tweet by Ilhan Omar, 11 February 2019. *https://twitter.com/IlhanMN/status/1095046561254567937.* Omar has since deleted her original 'Benjamins' tweet of 10 February.

6 Tweet by Ben Shapiro, 17 September 2015. *https://twitter.com/benshapiro/status/644505141299671041.*

7 Tweet by David Aaronovitch, 13 October 2018. *https://twitter.com/DAaronovitch/status/1051177385926770690.*

8 Tweet by Ben Shapiro, 15 April 2019. *https://twitter.com/
   benshapiro/status/1117867417831477248.*
9 *https://judas.watch/Alana_Lentin.*
10 Tweet by Suella Braverman, 3 April 2019. *https://twitter.
   com/SuellaBraverman/status/1113509478547300352.*
11 Tweet by Paul Embery, 7 April 2019. *https://twitter.com/
   paulembery/status/1114869646824562688?lang=en.*
12 Macron's statement should also be seen in the context of
   the adoption of the International Holocaust Remembrance
   Alliance definition of antisemitism by several states and
   by political parties, such as the British Labour Party,
   following much controversy, which, among other things,
   defines antisemitism as 'Denying the Jewish people their
   right to self-determination, e.g., by claiming that the
   existence of a State of Israel is a racist endeavor' and
   'Applying double standards by requiring of it a behavior
   not expected or demanded of any other democratic
   nation' (IHRA n.d.).
13 *Riposte laïque* 'About' page, *https://ripostelaique.com/
   qui-sommes-nous-2.*
14 Tweet by Josh Hammer, 14 April 2019. *https://twitter.
   com/josh_hammer/status/1117238067620982785.*

Conclusion: Talking and Not Talking about Race
1 *Indigènes* translates as 'indigenous' and is used provoca-
   tively by the decolonial activists of the *Parti des Indigènes
   de la République* (PIR) to recall the indigenizing of
   colonially dominated people under French rule.
2 LBC radio interview, 15 July 2018. *https://www.lbc.
   co.uk/radio/presenters/nigel-farage/steve-bannons-
   call-to-arms-fight-for-country/.*

References

20 Minutes. 2010. 'Kouchner s'attend à des critiques dans le monde sur l'interdiction du voile intégral en France.' 2 May. *https://www.20minutes.fr/france/401660-20100502-kouchner-attend-a-critiques-monde-interdiction-voile-integral-france*.

ABC Comedy. 2018. 'Lefty Boot Camp.' *Tonightly with Tom Ballard*. *https://www.youtube.com/watch?v=0lcYP_zOOXg*.

Abrams, Samuel J. 2018. 'Think Professors Are Liberal? Try School Administrators.' *The New York Times*, 19 October. *https://www.nytimes.com/2018/10/16/opinion/liberal-college-administrators.html*.

Agar, Nicholas. 2004. *Liberal Eugenics: In Defense of Human Enhancement*. New York: Blackwell.

Ahmed, Sara. 2004. 'Declarations of Whiteness: The Non-Performativity of Anti-Racism.' *Borderlands E-Journal* 3 (2). *http://www.borderlands.net.au/vol3no2_2004/ahmed_declarations.htm*.

Ahmed, Sara. 2012. *On Being Included: Racism and Diversity in Institutional Life*. Durham, NC: Duke University Press.

Ahmed, Sara. 2016. 'Progressive Racism.'

Feministkilljoys (blog), 30 May. *https://feminist-killjoys.com/2016/05/30/progressive-racism/*.

AIHW. N.d. 'Deaths in Australia, Life Expectancy.' Australian Institute of Health and Welfare. *https://www.aihw.gov.au/reports/life-expectancy-death/deaths/contents/life-expectancy*.

Allam, Lorena. 2018. 'All Children in Detention in the Northern Territory Are Indigenous.' *The Guardian*, 25 June. *https://www.theguardian.com/australia-news/2018/jun/25/all-children-in-detention-in-the-northern-territory-are-indigenous*.

Allam, Lorena. 2019. 'Indigenous Suicide: 35 Dead in Three Months, Including Three 12-Year-Old Children.' *The Guardian*, 21 March. *https://www.theguardian.com/australia-news/2019/mar/22/indigenous-suicide-35-dead-in-three-months-including-three-12-year-old-children*.

Andersson, Ruben. 2016. 'Hardwiring the Frontier? The Politics of Security Technology in Europe's 'Fight Against Illegal Migration.' *Security Dialogue* 47 (1): 22–39.

Andrews, Kehinde. 2018. 'The Challenge for Black Studies in the Neoliberal University.' In *Decolonising the University*, edited by Gurminder K. Bhambra, Kerem Nisancioglu, and Dalia Gebrial. London: Pluto Press.

Anidjar, Gil. 2003. *The Jew, the Arab: A History of the Enemy*. Stanford: Stanford University Press.

Anomaly, Jonathan. 2017. 'The Politics of Science: Why Scientists Might Not Say What the Evidence Supports.' *Quillette* (blog), 29 November. *https://quillette.com/2017/11/29/politics-science-scientists-might-not-say-evidence-supports/*.

Anomaly, Jonathan. 2018. 'Defending Eugenics: From Cryptic Choice to Conscious Selection.' *Monash Bioethics Review* 25: 24–35.

References

Antrosio, Jason. 2011. 'Race Reconciled Re-Debunks Race.' *Living Anthropologically* (blog), 5 June. *https://www.livinganthropologically.com/biological-anthropology/race-reconciled-debunks-race/*.

Antrosio, Jason. 2012. '"Social Construction of Race" = Conservative Goldmine.' *Living Anthropologically* (blog), 24 August. *https://www.livinganthropologically.com/social-construction-of-race/*.

Aouragh, Miriyam. 2019. '"White Privilege" and Shortcuts to Anti-Racism.' *Race & Class* 61 (2): 3–26.

Arendt, Hannah. 1951. *The Origins of Totalitarianism.* New York: Meridian.

Arruzza, Cinzia. 2016. 'Lessons from Italy: The Dangers of Anti-Trumpism.' Versobooks.com (blog), 21 November. *https://www.versobooks.com/blogs/2956-lessons-from-italy-the-dangers-of-anti-trumpism.*

Assoun, Simon. 2019. 'Simon, juif, antisioniste et gilet jaune.' 26 February. *https://www.liberation.fr/debats/2019/02/26/simon-juif-antisioniste-et-gilet-jaune_1711777.*

Balibar, Étienne. 1991. 'Racism and Nationalism.' In *Race, Nation, Class: Ambiguous Identities*, edited by Immanuel Maurice Wallerstein and Étienne Balibar. London: Verso.

Ball, Jared. 2014. 'Irreconcilable Anti-Blackness and Police Violence w Dr Frank Wilderson.' *Imixwhatilike!* (blog), 1 October. *https://imixwhatilike.org/2014/10/01/frankwildersonandantiblackness-2/.*

'Bandung du Nord.' 2018. 'Bandung du Nord: vers une internationale décoloniale.' *http://bandungdunord.webflow.io/.*

Barenblat, Rachel. 2018. 'Is Ranting Against "Globalism" Anti-Semitic?' *The Forward*, 24 October. *https://forward.com/scribe/412627/globalism-anti-semitism/.*

References

Barker, Martin. 1982. *The New Racism: Conservatives and the Ideology of the Tribe*. Frederick, MD: University Publications of America.

Batty, David. 2019. 'University Racism Study Criticised for Including Anti-White Harassment.' *The Guardian*, 23 October. *https://www.theguardian.com/world/2019/oct/23/university-racism-study-criticised-including-anti-white-harassment*.

Bayoumi, Moustafa. 2017. 'What's a "Lone Wolf"? It's the Special Name We Give White Terrorists.' *The Guardian*, 4 October. *https://www.theguardian.com/commentisfree/2017/oct/04/lone-wolf-white-terrorist-las-vegas*.

BBC News. 2019. 'Ofcom Investigates Snow "White People" Remark.' 8 April. *https://www.bbc.com/news/uk-47856058*.

Beckett, Lois. 2019. 'Students Burn Latina Author's Book After She Discusses White Privilege.' *The Guardian*, 13 October. *https://www.theguardian.com/books/2019/oct/13/students-burn-book-latina-author-jennine-capo-crucet*.

Bentouhami, Hourya. 2018. 'Pour une défense de l'antiracisme politique et de la démocratie.' Club de Mediapart, 15 January. *https://blogs.mediapart.fr/hourya-bentouhami/blog/150118/pour-une-defense-de-l-antiracisme-politique-et-de-la-*.

Bhambra, Gurminder K. 2017. 'Brexit, Trump, and "Methodological Whiteness": On the Misrecognition of Race and Class.' *The British Journal of Sociology* 68 (S1): S214–32.

Bhambra, Gurminder K., Kerem Nisancioglu, and Dalia Gebrial. 2018. *Decolonising the University*. London: Pluto Press.

190

Bhandar, Brenna. 2018. *Colonial Lives of Property: Law, Land, and Racial Regimes of Ownership.* Durham, NC: Duke University Press.

Bhattacharyya, Gargi. 2018. *Rethinking Racial Capitalism: Questions of Reproduction and Survival.* Lanham, MD: Rowman & Littlefield.

Bhattacharyya, Gargi. 2020. 'Revisiting "Common-Sense" in a Time of Cultivated Ignorance – a Conversation with Errol Lawrence.' *Identities: Global Studies in Culture and Power* 27 (1): 114–31.

Bkouche, Rudolf. 2015. 'Du philosémitisme d'état.' UJFP, 27 April. *https://www.ujfp.org/spip.php?article 4117&lang=fr.*

Blades, Lincoln Anthony. 2018. 'The FBI's "Black Identity Extremist" Classification Is Dangerous.' *Teen Vogue*, 30 April. *https://www.teenvogue.com/story/ why-the-fbis-black-identity-extremist-classification-is-dangerous.*

Blight, Daniel C. 2019. 'How Do White People See?' *Vogue Italia*, 31 October. *https://www.vogue.it/ fotografia/article/how-do-white-people-see.*

Boas, Franz. 2015a [1911]. *The Mind of Primitive Man.* London: Forgotten Books.

Bond, Chelsea. 2018. 'A White Woman Took My Baby.' *IndigenousX* (blog), 20 March. *https://indigenousx. com.au/chelsea-bond-a-white-woman-took-my-baby/.*

Bonilla-Silva, Eduardo. 2018. *Racism without Racists: Color-Blind Racism and the Persistence of Racial Inequality in America.* Lanham, MD: Rowman & Littlefield.

Bonnett, Alastair. 2000. *Anti-Racism.* London: Routledge.

Boochani, Behrouz. 2018. 'Five Years in Manus Purgatory.' *The Saturday Paper*, 29 September.

https://www.thesaturdaypaper.com.au/news/politics/ 2018/09/29/five-years-manus-purgatory/ 15381432006928.

Boucher, Manuel. 2018. 'La gauche et la "race": ambivalences et connivences.' *Figaro*, 26 December. *http:// www.lefigaro.fr/vox/societe/2018/12/26/31003- 20181226ARTFIG00092-la-gauche-et-la-race- ambivalences-et-connivences.php.*

Bouteldja, Houria. 2015. 'Racisme (s) et philosémitisme d'état ou comment politiser l'antiracisme en France ?' Parti des Indigènes de la République, 11 March. *http://indigenes-republique.fr/racisme-s-et-philosem- itisme-detat-ou-comment-politiser-lantiracisme-en- france-3/.*

Bouteldja, Houria. 2016. *Les Blancs, les Juifs et nous: vers une politique de l'amour révolutionnaire.* Paris: La Fabrique éditions.

Bouteldja, Houria, and Alana Lentin. 2019. 'We Are Not at Place de La République Because ...' OpenDemocracy, 28 February. *https://www. opendemocracy.net/en/can-europe-make-it/we-are- not-at-place-de-la-r-publique-because/.*

Boyer, Dave. 2018. 'Trump Declares Himself "Nationalist" Defending US Against "Power-Hungry Globalists".' *The Washington Times*, 22 October. *https://www.washingtontimes.com/news/2018/oct/22/ donald-trump-ted-cruz-rally-declares-himself-natio/.*

Breland, Ali. 2017. 'How White Engineers Built Racist Code – and Why It's Dangerous for Black People.' *The Guardian*, 4 December. *https://www.theguardian. com/technology/2017/dec/04/racist-facial-recog- nition-white-coders-black-people-police.*

Brigaudeau, Christel. 2019. 'Port du voile: le Sénat vote l'interdiction des signes religieux lors des sorties scolaires.' *Le Parisien*, 29 October 2019. *http://*

www.leparisien.fr/societe/port-du-voile-le-senat-vote-l-interdiction-des-signes-religieux-lors-des-sorties-scolaires-29-10-2019-8182914.php.

Brodkin, Karen. 1999. *How Did Jews Become White Folks and What Does That Say about Race in America?* New Brunswick, NJ: Rutgers University Press.

Brown, Katy, Aaron Winter, and Aurelien Mondon. 2019. '"Populist" Can Be a Weasel Word for "Racist", and That's Dangerous.' Open Democracy, 16 October 2019. *https://www.opendemocracy.net/en/opendemocracyuk/populist-can-be-a-weasel-word-for-racist-and-thats-dangerous/?fbclid=IwAR1X6Yj1FQQVTqqCTZZgKHcYS2fTw8tnPvSjdcQ3bsE2r3WXVYdOjPjD0Bo.*

Brown, Wendy. 1995. *States of Injury: Power and Freedom in Late Modernity*. Princeton, NJ: Princeton University Press.

Browne, Simone. 2015. *Dark Matters: On the Surveillance of Blackness*. Durham, NC: Duke University Press.

Bruckner, Pascal. 2012. *The Tyranny of Guilt: An Essay on Western Masochism*. Princeton, NJ: Princeton University Press.

Bruney, Gabrielle. 2019. 'Trump Called Religious and Racial Minority Members of Congress "Savages" on Twitter.' *Esquire*, 28 September. *https://www.esquire.com/news-politics/a29279632/donald-trump-savages-aoc-schiff-nadler/.*

Buchan, Lizzy. 2019. 'Jacob Rees-Mogg Faces Sacking Calls after Soros Remark "Straight from the Far-Right's Antisemitic Playbook".' *The Independent*, 4 October. *https://www.independent.co.uk/news/uk/politics/jacob-rees-mogg-antisemitism-george-soros-lord-dubs-boris-johnson-a9142756.html.*

References

Bunzl, Matti. 2007. *Anti-Semitism and Islamophobia: Hatreds Old and New in Europe*. Chicago: Prickly Paradigm Press.

Burack, Emily. 2018. 'Everything You Need to Know about Britain's Current Anti-Semitism Debate.' *Alma*, 19 April. *https://www.heyalma.com/everything-need-know-britain-current-anti-semitism-debate/*.

Burden-Stelly, Charisse. 2016. 'The Modern Capitalist State and the Black Challenge: Culturalism and the Elision of Political Economy.' Dissertation. *http://digitalassets.lib.berkeley.edu/etd/ucb/text/BurdenStelly_berkeley_0028E_15992.pdf*.

Burrows, Don M. 2015. 'There Is No "Judeo-Christian Tradition".' *Patheos*, 20 November. *https://www.patheos.com/blogs/unfundamentalist christians/2015/11/there-is-no-judeo-christian-tradition/*.

Busby, Mattha. 2019. 'Tommy Robinson Released from Jail After Nine Weeks.' *The Guardian*, 13 September. *https://www.theguardian.com/uk-news/2019/sep/13/tommy-robinson-released-jail*.

Butler, Judith. 1998. 'Merely Cultural.' *New Left Review* 227: 33–44.

Butler, Judith. 2006. *Gender Trouble*. New York: Routledge.

Byrd, Jodi A. 2011. *The Transit of Empire: Indigenous Critiques of Colonialism*. Minneapolis: University of Minnesota Press.

Caldwell, Christopher. 2009. *Reflections on the Revolution in Europe: Can Europe Be the Same with Different People in It?* London: Allen Lane.

Camus, Renaud. 2015. *Le grand remplacement*. Paris: David Reinharc.

Carey, Benedict. 2018. 'Can We Really Inherit Trauma?'. *The New York Times*, 10 December. *https://www.*

nytimes.com/2018/12/10/health/mind-epigenetics-genes.html.

Carmichael, Stokely, and Charles V. Hamilton. 1969. *Black Power.* Harmondsworth: Penguin.

Carter, Robert. 2007. 'Genes, Genomes and Genealogies: The Return of Scientific Racism.' *Ethnic and Racial Studies* 30 (4): 546–56.

Cartledge, Paul. 2019. 'The Left-Behind v. the Metropolitan Elite? That's a Lazy, Harmful Cliché.' *The Guardian*, 12 April. *https://www.theguardian.com/commentisfree/2019/apr/12/left-behind-v-metropolitan-elite-harmful-cliche.*

CCCS. 2014 [1982]. *The Empire Strikes Back: Race and Racism in 70s Britain.* London: Routledge.

Césaire, Aimé. 2000 [1955]. *Discourse on Colonialism*, trans. Joan Pinkham. New York: Monthly Review Press.

Chotiner, Isaac. 2019. 'A Political Scientist Defends White Identity Politics.' *The New Yorker*, 30 April. *https://www.newyorker.com/news/q-and-a/a-political-scientist-defends-white-identity-politics-eric-kaufmann-whiteshift-book.*

Chrenoff, Arthur. 2019. 'Who Says We Shouldn't Speak about "Cultural Marxism"?' *The Spectator Australia*, 28 March. *https://www.spectator.com.au/2019/03/who-says-we-shouldnt-speak-about-cultural-marxism/.*

Chun, Wendy Hui Kyong. 2012. 'Race and/as Technology, or How to Do Things to Race.' In *Race After the Internet*, edited by Lisa Nakamura and Peter A. Chow-White. London: Routledge.

Collins, Patricia Hill. 2000. *Black Feminist Thought Knowledge, Consciousness, and the Politics of Empowerment.* New York: Routledge.

The Combahee River Collective. 1977. 'The Combahee

River Collective Statement.' *http://circuitous.org/ scraps/combahee.html.*

Confiant, Raphael. 2008. '"Souschiens" ou "sous-chiens": une (sombre) histoire de Tiret.' *Montray Kreyol,* 12 June. *http://www.montraykreyol.org/ article/souchiens-ou-sous-chiens-une-sombre-histoire-de-tiret.*

Coulthard, Glen Sean. 2017. *Red Skin, White Masks: Rejecting the Colonial Politics of Recognition.* Minneapolis: University of Minnesota Press.

Da Silva, Chantal. 2019. 'Barack Obama Says Not "Everyone Who Is Disturbed by Migration" Should Be Labeled "Racist"'. *Newsweek,* 8 April. *https:// www.newsweek.com/barack-obama-says-not-everyone-who-disturbed-migration-can-be-branded-racist-1388642.*

Dale, Helen. 2018. 'Australia's Mistress of the Intellectual Dark Web.' *The Spectator,* 2 June. *https://www.spectator.co.uk/2018/06/australias-mistress-of-the-intellectual-dark-web/.*

Davis, D. A. 2007. 'Narrating the Mute: Racializing and Racism in a Neoliberal Moment.' *Souls, A Critical Journal of Black Politics, Culture & Society* 9 (4): 346–60.

Davis, Kira. 2019. 'Liam Neeson's Racism Confession Is Actually the Beginning of a Very Important Conversation.' Townhall, 5 February. *https:// townhall.com/columnists/kiradavis/2019/02/05/ liam-neesons-racism-confession-is-actually-the-beginning-of-a-very-important-conver sation-n2540783.*

Dawkins, Richard. 2016 [1976]. *The Selfish Gene: 40th Anniversary Edition.* Oxford: Oxford University Press.

Deutsche Welle. 2019. 'Germany: Halle Suspect Confesses to Yom Kippur Shooting.'

DW.com, 11 October. *https://www.dw.com/en/germany-halle-suspect-confesses-to-yom-kippur-shooting/a-50791324.*

Di Angelo, Robin. 2018. *White Fragility: Why It's So Hard for White People to Talk about Racism.* London: Penguin.

Dickson, E. J. 2019. 'Mysterious Deaths Leave Ferguson Activists "On Pins and Needles".' *Rolling Stone,* 18 March. *https://www.rollingstone.com/culture/culture-news/ferguson-death-mystery-black-lives-matter-michael-brown-809407/.*

Dodson, Shannan. 2019. 'Why Is It More Offensive To Call Someone Racist Than To Say Something Racist?' *10 Daily,* 29 January. *https://tendaily.com.au/views/a190129kph/why-is-it-more-offensive-to-call-someone-racist-than-to-say-something-racist-20190129.*

Dorling, Daniel, and Sally Tomlinson. 2019. *Rule Britannia: Brexit and the End of Empire.* London: Biteback Publishing.

Du Bois, W. E. B. 1940. *Dusk of Dawn: An Essay Toward an Autobiography of a Race Concept.* Oxford: Oxford University Press.

Dzodan, Flavia. 2016. 'A Simplified Political History of Big Data.' *This Political Woman* (blog), 16 December. *https://medium.com/this-political-woman/a-simplified-political-history-of-data-26935bdc5082.*

Dzodan, Flavia. 2017. 'From Gut Feeling to Policy: The Lifecycle of Hate.' *This Political Woman* (blog), 2 August 2017. *https://medium.com/this-political-woman/from-gut-feeling-to-policy-the-lifecycle-of-hate-61d9a330cfe7.*

Eaton, George. 2019. 'Roger Scruton: "Cameron's Resignation Was the Death Knell of the Conservative Party".' *The News Statesman,* 10 April 2019.

References

https://www.newstatesman.com/politics/uk/2019/04/ roger-scruton-cameron-s-resignation-was-death- knell-conservative-party.

Eddo-Lodge, Reni. 2018. 'Political Blackness.' *About Race with Reni Eddo-Lodge* (podcast), 12 April. *https://www.aboutracepodcast.com/4-political- blackness.*

El-Enany, Nadine. 2016. 'Brexit as Nostalgia for Empire.' *Critical Legal Thinking* (blog), 19 June. *http://criticallegalthinking.com/2016/06/19/ brexit-nostalgia-empire/.*

El-Haj, Nadia Abu. 2007. 'The Genetic Reinscription of Race.' *Annual Review of Anthropology* 36 (1): 283–300.

Erel, Umut, Karim Murji, and Zaki Nahaboo. 2016. 'Understanding the Contemporary Race–Migration Nexus.' *Ethnic and Racial Studies* 39 (8): 1339–60.

Evans, Gavin. 2018. 'The Unwelcome Revival of "Race Science".' *The Guardian*, 2 March. *http:// www.theguardian.com/news/2018/mar/02/ the-unwelcome-revival-of-race-science.*

Evon, Dan. 2016. 'Fact Check: Rothschild Family Wealth.' Snopes.Com, 30 October. *https://www. snopes.com/fact-check/rothschild-family-wealth/.*

Fanon, Frantz. 1986 [1967]. *Black Skin, White Masks*, trans. Charles Lam Markmann. London: Pluto Press.

Fanon, Frantz. 2007 [1965]. *A Dying Colonialism*, trans. Haakon Chevalier. New York: Grove Press.

Fanon, Frantz. 2018. *Alienation and Freedom*, ed. Jean Khalfa and Robert C. Young, trans. Steven Corcoran. London: Bloomsbury.

Favell, Adrian. 2003. 'Integration Nations: The Nation-State and Research on Migration in Western Europe.' In *International Migration Research: Constructions, Omissions, and the Promises of Interdisciplinarity,* edited by Michael Bommes and Eva T. Morawska. London: Ashgate.

Favell, Adrian. 2008. 'The New Face of East–West Migration in Europe.' *Journal of Ethnic and Migration Studies* 34 (5): 701–16.

Feertchak, Alexis. 2018. 'Finkielkraut, Onfray, Michéa: ces intellectuels qui portent le "gilet jaune".' *Figaro*, 30 November. *http://www.lefigaro.fr/actualite-france/2018/11/30/01016-20181130ARTFIG00335-finkielkraut-onfray-michea-ces-intellectuels-qui-portent-le-gilet-jaune.php*.

Ferguson, Niall. 2004. *Empire: The Rise and Demise of the British World Order and the Lessons for Global Power*. New York: Basic Books.

Fernando, Mayanthi, and Vincent Lloyd. 2018. 'Whites, Jews, and Us.' *The Immanent Frame. https://tif.ssrc.org/category/exchanges/book-blog/book-forums/whites-jews-us/*.

Fields, Karen E., and Barbara J. Fields. 2012. *Racecraft: The Soul of Inequality in American Life*. London: Verso.

Fields, Karen E., Barbara J. Fields, and Jason Farbman. 2015. 'How Race Is Conjured.' *Jacobin*, June. *https://www. jacobinmag.com/2015/06/karen-barbara-fields-racecraft-dolezal-racism/*.

Folayan, Sabaah, and Damon Davis (dir.). 2017. *Whose Streets?* Documentary.

Foley, Wendy. 2005. 'Tradition and Change in Urban Indigenous Food Practices.' *Postcolonial Studies* 8 (1): 25–44.

Foner, Nancy, Jan Rath, Jan Willem Duyvendak, and Rogier van Reekum. 2014. *New York and Amsterdam: Immigration and the New Urban Landscape*. New York: New York University Press.

Foucault, Michel. 2003. *'Society Must Be Defended'*:

Lectures at the Collège de France, 1975–76, trans. David Macey. London: Penguin

Fraser, Nancy. 2017. 'From Progressive Neoliberalism to Trump – and Beyond.' *American Affairs Journal* 1 (4). *https://americanaffairsjournal.org/2017/11/progressive-neoliberalism-trump-beyond/*.

Freelon, Dean, Charlton McIlwain, and Meredith Clark. 2016. 'Beyond the Hashtags: #Ferguson, #Blacklivesmatter, and the Online Struggle for Offline Justice.' Center for Media and Social Impact, American University, 15 March. *https://doi.org/10.2139/ssrn.2747066*.

Friedersdorf, Conor. 2019. 'Ilhan Omar Falls Victim to the Outrage Exhibitionists.' *The Atlantic*, 13 April. *https://www.theatlantic.com/ideas/archive/2019/04/ilhan-omar/586993/*.

Fryer, Brooke. 2019a. 'Indigenous Youth Suicide at Crisis Point' NITV, 15 January. *https://www.sbs.com.au/nitv/article/2019/01/15/indigenous-youth-suicide-crisis-point*.

Fryer, Brooke. 2019b. 'No DNA Test Exists for Aboriginality: Scientists.' NITV, 16 March. *https://www.sbs.com.au/nitv/article/2019/03/16/no-dna-test-exists-aboriginality-scientists1*.

Gander, Kashmira. 2015. 'Britain First Wants the Media to Stop Using the Word "Racism".' *The Independent*, 15 January. *https://www.independent.co.uk/news/uk/home-news/britain-first-wants-the-media-to-stop-using-the-word-racism-a6738811.html*.

Garcia, J.L.A. 1999. 'Philosophical Analysis and the Moral Concept of Racism.' *Philosophy & Social Criticism* 25 (5): 1–32.

Garcia-Rojas, Claudia. 2016. 'The Surveillance of Blackness: From the Trans-Atlantic Slave Trade to Contemporary Surveillance Technologies.' *Truthout*, 3

March. *https://truthout.org/articles/the-surveillance-of-blackness-from-the-slave-trade-to-the-police/*.

Garratt, Patrick. 2019. 'Herbert Marcuse and "Cultural Marxism".' Versobooks.com (blog), 29 April. *https://www.versobooks.com/blogs/4285-herbert-marcuse-and-cultural-marxism*.

Gartrell, Adam. 2018. 'Malcolm Turnbull Defends "Great Australian" Jim Molan from Racism Claims.' *The Sydney Morning Herald*, 6 February. *https://www.smh.com.au/politics/federal/jim-molan-agrees-race-hate-group-is-appalling-but-won-t-remove-posts-20180206-p4yzh2.html*.

Gillard, Chris. 2018. 'Friction-Free Racism.' *Real Life*, 15 October. *https://reallifemag.com/friction-free-racism/?fbclid=IwAR2ilvxROY1bqPP1k-iqU5i9FhBN-vWRk5NlvH_CusiQHStEN9KGp7ykmJRQ*.

Gilroy, Paul. 2001. *Against Race: Imagining Political Culture beyond the Color Line*. Cambridge, MA: Harvard University Press.

Girard, Étienne, and Hadrien Mathoux. 2019. 'L'offensive Des Obsédés de La Race, Du Sexe, Du Genre, de l'identité....' *Marianne*, 11 April. *https://www.marianne.net/societe/l-offensive-des-obsedes-de-la-race-du-sexe-du-genre-de-l-identite*.

Glickman, Lawrence B. 2018. 'The Racist Politics of the English Language.' *Boston Review*, 20 November. *http://bostonreview.net/race/lawrence-glickman-racially-tinged*.

Glosser, David. 2018. 'Stephen Miller Is an Immigration Hypocrite. I Know Because I'm His Uncle.' *Politico Magazine*, 13 August. *https://www.politico.com/magazine/story/2018/08/13/stephen-miller-is-an-immigration-hypocrite-i-know-because-im-his-uncle-219351*.

Goldberg, David Theo. 1990. 'Racism and Rationality:

The Need for a New Critique.' *Philosophy of Science* 20 (2): 317–50.

Goldberg, David Theo. 2009. *The Threat of Race: Reflections on Racial Neoliberalism*. Malden, MA: Blackwell.

Goldberg, David Theo. 2011. *The Racial State*. Malden, MA: Blackwell.

Goldberg, David Theo. 2015. 'Racial Comparisons, Relational Racisms: Some Thoughts on Method.' In *Theories of Race and Ethnicity: Contemporary Debates and Perspectives*, edited by Karim Murji and John Solomos. Cambridge: Cambridge University Press.

Golub, Alex. 2014. 'Geneticists Think Nicholas Wade's "A Troublesome Inheritance" Is Wrong.' *Savage Minds*, 11 August. *https://savageminds.org/2014/08/11/geneticists-think-nicholas-wades-a-troublesome-inheritance-is-wrong/*.

Goodfellow, Maya. 2019. 'To Fix Its Problems Now, Labour Must Face the Racism in Its Past.' *The Guardian*, 8 March. *https://www.theguardian.com/commentisfree/2019/mar/08/labour-party-racism-truth-past*.

Goodhart, David. 2004. 'Too Diverse?' *Prospect Magazine*, 20 February. *https://www.prospectmagazine.co.uk/magazine/too-diverse-david-goodhart-multiculturalism-britain-immigration-globalisation*.

Goodhart, David. 2017a. *The Road to Somewhere : The Populist Revolt and the Future of Politics*. London: Hurst.

Goodhart, David. 2017b. 'White Self-Interest Is Not Same Thing as Racism.' Policy Exchange, 3 March. *https://policyexchange.org.uk/white-self-interest-is-not-same-thing-as-racism/*.

Goodwin, Matthew. 2018. 'National Populism Is

Unstoppable – and the Left Still Doesn't Understand Why.' *The Guardian*, 8 November. *https://www. theguardian.com/commentisfree/2018/nov/08/ national-populism-immigration-financial-crisis-globalisation.*

Gordon, Lewis R. 1999. *Bad Faith and Antiblack Racism.* Amherst, NY: Humanity Books.

Gordon, Lewis R. 2016. 'Rarely Kosher: Studying Jews of Color in North America.' *American Jewish History* 100 (1): 105–16.

Gordon, Lewis R. 2018a. 'Critical Reflections on Afropessimism by Lewis R. Gordon.' *The Brotherwise Dispatch* (blog), 6 June. *http://brotherwisedispatch. blogspot.com/2018/06/critical-reflections-on-afropes simism.html.*

Gordon, Lewis R. 2018b. 'Pourquoi les juifs ne doivent pas redouter la libération.' *Tumultes* 50: 97–108.

Gravlee, Clarence C. 2009. 'How Race Becomes Biology: Embodiment of Social Inequality.' *American Journal of Physical Anthropology* 139 (1): 47–57.

Grey, Sara, and Joe Cleffie. 2015. 'Peter Singer's Race Problem.' *Jacobin*, 6 August. *http:// jacobinmag.com/2015/08/animal-rights-cecil-the-lion-peter-singer-speciesism/.*

Grosfoguel, Ramón. 2015. 'Epistemic Racism/Sexism, Westernized Universities and the Four Genocides/ Epistemicides of the Long Sixteenth Century.' In *Eurocentrism, Racism and Knowledge*, edited by Marta Araújo and Silvia Rodriguez Maeso. London: Palgrave Macmillan.

Grosfoguel, Ramón, Eric Melants, Philomena Essed, and Kwame Nimako. 2006. 'Designs and (Co)Incidents: Cultures of Scholarship and Public Policy on Immigrants/ Minorities in the Netherlands.' *International Journal of Comparative Sociology.* 47 (3–4): 281–312.

References

Grzanka, Patrick R., Jenny Dyck Brian, and Janet K. Shim. 2016. 'My Bioethics Will Be Intersectional or It Will Be [Bleep].' *The American Journal of Bioethics* 16 (4): 27–29.

Guinier, Lani. 2004. 'From Racial Liberalism to Racial Literacy: *Brown v. Board of Education* and the Interest-Divergence Dilemma.' *Journal of American History* 91 (1): 92–118.

Haaretz. 2015. 'Netanyahu: Hitler Didn't Want to Exterminate the Jews.' *Haaretz*, 21 October. *https://www.haaretz.com/israel-news/netanyahu-absolves-hitler-of-guilt-1.5411578*.

Hacking, Ian. 2003. *The Social Construction of What?* Cambridge: Cambridge University Press.

Haider, Asad. 2018a. *Mistaken Identity: Race and Class in the Age of Trump*. London: Verso.

Haider, Asad. 2018b. 'Organizing Histories.' *Viewpoint Magazine*, 19 June. *https://www.viewpointmag.com/2018/06/19/organizing-histories/*.

Hall, Catherine. 2013. 'Britain's Massive Debt to Slavery.' *The Guardian*, 27 February. *https://www.theguardian.com/commentisfree/2013/feb/27/britain-debt-slavery-made-public*.

Hall, Stuart. 1980. 'Race, Articulation and Societies Structured in Dominance.' In *Sociological Theories: Race and Colonialism*. Paris: UNESCO.

Hall, Stuart. 2017. *The Fateful Triangle: Race, Ethnicity, Nation*. Cambridge, MA: Harvard University Press.

Hamade, Houssam, and Nancy Fraser. 2017. 'A New Leftist Narrative Is Required.' Open Democracy, 8 August. *https://www.opendemocracy.net/en/new-leftist-narrative-is-required/*.

Harris, Cheryl I. 1993. 'Whiteness as Property.' *Harvard Law Review* 106 (8): 1709–91.

Hartigan, John. 2008. 'Is Race Still Socially Constructed?

The Recent Controversy over Race and Medical Genetics.' *Science as Culture* 17 (2): 163–93.

Hesse, Barnor. 2004. 'Im/Plausible Deniability: Racism's Conceptual Double Bind.' *Social Identities* 10 (1): 9–29.

Hesse, Barnor. 2011. 'Self-Fulfilling Prophecy: The Postracial Horizon.' *South Atlantic Quarterly* 110 (155–78).

Hesse, Barnor. 2013. 'Raceocracy: How the Racial Exception Proves the Racial Rule.' Irving K. Barber Learning Centre, University of British Columbia, 7 March. *https://ikblc.ubc.ca/barnorhesse/*.

Hesse, Barnor. 2014. 'Racism's Alterity: The After-Life of Black Sociology.' In *Racism and Sociology*, edited by Wulf D. Hund and Alana Lentin. Racism Analysis – Series B: Yearbooks. Berlin: Lit Verlag.

Hesse, Barnor. 2016. 'Preface: Counter Racial Formation Theory.' In *Conceptual Aphasia in Black: Displacing Racial Formation*, edited by P. Khalil Saucier and Tryon P. Woods. Lanham, MD: Rowman & Littlefield.

Hinsliff, Gaby. 2017. '*The Strange Death of Europe* by Douglas Murray Review – Gentrified Xenophobia.' *The Guardian*, 6 May. *https://www.theguardian.com/books/2017/may/06/strange-death-europe-immigration-xenophobia*.

Hirsch, Robert. 2019. 'Les gilets jaunes et les juifs.' Club de Mediapart, 15 February. *https://blogs.mediapart.fr/robert-hirsch/blog/150219/les-gilets-jaunes-et-les-juifs*.

Hochschild, Joshua P. 2019. 'Taleb's Call to Duel.' *First Things*, 5 August. *https://www.firstthings.com/web-exclusives/2019/08/talebs-call-to-duel*.

hooks, bell. 1995. *Killing Rage, Ending Racism*. London: Penguin.

Human Rights Law Centre. 2019. 'Overview of the

Colonial Inquest into the Death of Tanya Day.'
https://www.hrlc.org.au/tanya-day-overview.

Hume, Tim. 2019. 'Hungarian Fascists Attacked a Jewish Community Center. It's Not the First Time.' *Vice*, 24 October. *https://www.vice.com/en_us/article/ mbm45x/hungarian-fascists-attacked-a-jewish- ommunity-center-its-not-the-first-time*.

Hund, Wulf D. 2018. 'Fragments from the History of "Racism" [Version 17].' *https://www.academia. edu/37368498/Fragments_from_the_History_of_ Racism_Version_17_*.

Ignatiev, Noel. 2015. *How the Irish Became White*. London and New York: Routledge.

IHRA. N.d. 'Working Definition of Antisemitism.' International Holocaust Remembrance Alliance. *https://www.holocaustremembrance.com/ working-definition-antisemitism*.

Illing, Sean. 2019. 'White Identity Politics Is about More than Racism.' *Vox*, 26 April. *https://www.vox.com/2019/4/26/18306125/ white-identity-politics-trump-racism-ashley-jardina*.

IOM. 2019. 'Mediterranean Migrant Arrivals Reach 29,844 in 2019; Deaths Reach 681.' International Organization for Migration, 5 July. *https://www. iom.int/news/mediterranean-migrant-arrivals-reach- 29844-2019-deaths-reach-681*.

Jardina, Ashley. 2019. *White Identity Politics*. Cambridge: Cambridge University Press.

Jivraj, Suhraiya. 2019. 'Why Are Students Having the "Uncomfortable" Conversations about Race?' *Times Higher Education* (THE) (blog), 20 October. *https://www.timeshighereducation.com/blog/ why-are-students-having-uncomfortable-conversa tions-about-race*.

Johnson, Rhiannon. 2018. 'Canada Research Chair

Critical of US Senator's DNA Claim to Indigenous Identity.' CBC, 15 October. *https://www.cbc.ca/news/indigenous/kim-tallbear-elizabeth-warren-dna-results-indigenous-identity-1.4863903.*

Joskowicz, Ari. 2014. *The Modernity of Others: Jewish Anti-Catholicism in Germany and France.* Stanford: Stanford University Press.

Judaken, Jonathan. 2018. 'Introduction.' *The American Historical Review* 123 (4): 1122–38.

Karp, Paul. 2019. 'Scott Morrison Gave "Negative Globalism" Speeches without Consulting Dfat.' *The Guardian*, 24 October. *https://www.theguardian.com/australia-news/2019/oct/25/scott-morrison-gave-negative-globalism-speeches-without-consulting-dfat.*

Katz, Ethan B. 2018. 'An Imperial Entanglement: Anti-Semitism, Islamophobia, and Colonialism.' *American Historical Review* 123 (4): 1190–209.

Kauanui, J. Kēhaulani. 2016. '"A Structure, Not an Event": Settler Colonialism and Enduring Indigeneity.' *Lateral: Journal of the Cultural Studies Association* 5 (1). *https://doi.org/10.25158/L5.1.7.*

Kaufmann, Eric. 2017. *'Racial Self-Interest' Is Not Racism: Ethno-Demographic Interests and the Immigration Debate.* Policy Exchange. *https://policyexchange.org.uk/wp-content/uploads/2017/03/Racial-Self-Interest-is-not-Racism-FINAL.pdf.*

Kaufmann, Eric. 2018a. *Whiteshift: Populism, Immigration and the Future of White Majorities.* London: Penguin.

Kaufmann, Eric. 2018b. 'Taking on the Social Justice Warriors.' *UnHerd*, 20 December. *https://unherd.com/2018/12/taking-on-the-social-justice-warriors/.*

Kaufmann, Eric. 2019. 'How the Woke Inquisition Broke Cambridge.' *UnHerd*, 2 May. *https://*

unherd.com/2019/05/how-the-woke-inquisition-broke-cambridge/.

Kekatos, Mary. 2018. 'Black Michigan Teen Nearly Shot after Missing His Bus and Knocking on a Door Asking for Directions.' *Daily Mail*, 13 April. *https://www.dailymail.co.uk/news/article-5613813/Black-Michigan-teen-nearly-shot-missing-bus-knocking-door-asking-directions.html*.

Kellermann, Nathan P. F. 2013. 'Epigenetic Transmission of Holocaust Trauma: Can Nightmares Be Inherited?' *Israel Journal of Psychiatry and Related Sciences: The Official Publication of the Israel Psychiatric Association* 50 (1): 33–7.

Kelley, Robin D.G. 2000. 'Foreword.' In *Black Marxism: The Making of the Black Radical Tradition* by Cedric J. Robinson. London: Pluto Press.

Kelley, Robin D. G. 2016. 'Black Study, Black Struggle.' *Boston Review*, 1 March. *http://bostonreview.net/forum/robin-d-g-kelley-black-study-black-struggle*.

Kelly, Vivienne. 2019. 'Studio 10 Cleared by Watchdog over Broadcasting Kerri-Anne Kennerley's Inflammatory Indigenous Comments.' *Mumbrella*, 5 October. *https://mumbrella.com.au/studio-10-cleared-by-watchdog-over-broadcasting-kerri-anne-kennerleys-inflammatory-indigenous-comments-601221*.

Kendzior, Sarah. 2016. 'Meet Darren Seals. Then Tell Me Black Death Is Not a Business.' *The Correspondent*, 1 October. *https://thecorrespondent.com/5349/meet-darren-seals-then-tell-me-black-death-is-not-a-business/1512965275833-fe73c5b1*.

Kerner, Ina. 2007. 'Challenges of Critical Whiteness Studies.' 13 October. *http://translate.eipcp.net/strands/03/kerner-strands01en/print.html*.

Kesvani, Hussein. 2019. 'Opinion: "Cultural Marxism"

Is a Far-Right Conspiracy in Murky Internet Forums – so Why Is a Tory MP Now Using It?' *The Independent*, 27 March. *https://www.independent.co.uk/voices/cultural-marxism-suella-braverman-conservative-mp-antisemitism-a8842806.html*.

Kirkup, Kristy. 2018. 'Indigenous Women Coerced into Sterilizations across Canada: Senator.' CBC, 12 November. *https://www.cbc.ca/news/politics/sterilization-indigenous-1.4902303*.

Kistka Z. A., L. Palomar, K. A. Lee, S. E. Boslaugh, M. F. Wangler, F. S. Cole, M. R. DeBaun, and L. J. Muglia. 2007. 'Racial Disparity in the Frequency of Recurrence of Preterm Birth.' *American Journal of Obstetrics and Gynecology* 196: 131.e1–131.e6.

Klug, Brian. 2014. 'The Limits of Analogy: Comparing Islamophobia and Antisemitism.' *Patterns of Prejudice* 48 (5): 442–59.

Knaus, Christopher. 2019. 'Murdoch University Sues Whistleblower After Comments on International Students.' *The Guardian*, 11 October. *https://www.theguardian.com/australia-news/2019/oct/11/murdoch-university-sues-whistleblower-after-comments-on-international-students*.

Koopmans, Ruud, and Paul Statham. 1999. 'Challenging the Liberal Nation-State? Postnationalism, Multiculturalism, and the Collective Claims-Making of Migrants and Ethnic Minorities in Britain and Germany.' *American Journal of Sociology* 105 (3): 652–96.

Kumar, Ashok, Dalia Gebrial, Adam Elliott-Cooper, and Shruti Iyer. 2018. 'Marxist Interventions into Contemporary Debates.' *Historical Materialism* 26 (2). *http://www.historicalmaterialism.org/articles/marxist-interventions-into-contemporary-debates*.

Kundnani, Arun. 2015. *The Muslims Are*

Coming! Islamophobia, Extremism, and the Domestic War on Terror. London: Verso.

La Trobe University. 2019. 'Has Racism in Contemporary Australia Entered the Political Mainstream?' *https://www.youtube.com/watch?v=shs2fJJarL4*.

Langbehn, Volker, and Mohammad Salama. 2011. *German Colonialism: Race, the Holocaust, and Postwar Germany*. New York: Columbia University Press.

Langmuir, Gavin L. 1993. *History, Religion, and Antisemitism*. Berkeley: University of California Press.

Le Point. 2018. 'Le "décolonialisme", une stratégie hégémonique: l'appel de 80 intellectuels.' *Le Point*, 28 November. *https://www.lepoint.fr/politique/le-decolonialisme-une-strategie-hegemonique-l-appel-de-80-intellectuels-28-11-2018-2275104_20.php*.

Leifer, Joshua. 2018. 'Tapping the "Hidden Spring" of Anti-Semitism in Orbán's Hungary.' *+972 Magazine* (blog), 12 October. *https://972mag.com/tapping-the-hidden-spring-of-anti-semitism-in-orbans-hungary/138149/*.

Lentin, Alana. 2008. 'Europe and the Silence about Race.' *European Journal of Social Theory* 11 (4): 487–503.

Lentin, Alana. 2014a. 'Post-Race, Post Politics: The Paradoxical Rise of Culture after Multiculturalism.' *Ethnic and Racial Studies* 37 (8): 1268–85.

Lentin, Alana. 2014b. 'Postracial Silences: The Othering of Race in Europe.' In *Racism and Sociology*, edited by Wulf D. Hund and Alana Lentin. Racism Analysis – Series B: Yearbooks, V. Berlin: Lit Verlag.

Lentin, Alana. 2016. 'Racism in Public or Public Racism: Doing Anti-Racism in "Post-Racial" Times.' *Ethnic and Racial Studies* 39 (1): 33–48.

Lentin, Alana. 2018. 'Beyond Denial: "Not Racism" as Racist Violence.' *Continuum* 32 (4): 400–14.

Lentin, Alana, and Gavan Titley. 2011. *The Crises of Multiculturalism: Racism in a Neoliberal Age.* London: Zed Books.

Lentin, Alana, and signatories. 2017. 'The Good Conscience of French Intellectuals: The Case of Thomas Guénolé and the French Left of Jean-Luc Mélenchon. An Open Letter.' *Open Democracy,* 14 December. *https://www.opendemocracy.net/en/can-europe-make-it/good-conscience-of-french-intellectuals-case-of-thomas-gu/.*

Lentin, Ronit. 2018. *Traces of Racial Exception: Racializing Israeli Settler Colonialism.* London: Bloomsbury.

Levin, Bess. 2018. 'Trump: "A Lot of People Say" George Soros Is Funding the Migrant Caravan.' *Vanity Fair,* 31 October. *https://www.vanityfair.com/news/2018/10/donald-trump-george-soros-caravan.*

Levitz, Eric. 2019. 'If You Are Defending Stephen Miller, You Are an Ally of Anti-Semitism.' *Intelligencer,* 9 April. *http://nymag.com/intelligencer/2019/04/ilhan-omar-is-right-stephen-miller-is-a-white-nationalist.html.*

Lévy, Bernard-Henri. 2016. 'Taking Sides in the War within Islam.' BHL, 20 April. *http://www.bernard-henri-levy.com/taking-sides-in-the-war-within-islam-bhl-monde-50087.html.*

Lévy, Bernard-Henri. 2017. 'A Conversation with Bernard-Henri Lévy.' Interview by Ann Louise Bardach. *Los Angeles Review of Books,* 18 January. *https://lareviewofbooks.org/article/conversation-bernard-henri-levy/.*

Lewontin, Richard. 2006. 'Confusions about Human Races.' Social Science Research Council, 7 June. *http://raceandgenomics.ssrc.org/Lewontin/.*

Lilla, Mark. 2016. 'The End of Identity Liberalism'

References

New York Times, 20 November. *https://www.nytimes. com/2016/11/20/opinion/sunday/the-end-of-identity- liberalism.html*.

Loomes, Phoebe, and Stephanie Bedo. 2019. 'Massive Crowds Protest at Invasion Day Rallies across Australia.' NewsComAu, 26 January. *https://www. news.com.au/national/massive-crowds-protest-at- invasion-day-rallies-across-australia/news-story/ aa73dc94f88b4ccb84f0694728ec68ef#.icxo1*.

Lorde, Audre. 1978. 'A Litany for Survival.' *https://www.poetryfoundation.org/ poems/147275/a-litany-for-survival*.

Lorde, Audre. 1981. 'The Uses of Anger: Women Responding to Racism.' Presented at the National Women's Studies Association Conference, Storrs, CT.

Lorde, Audre. 2017. *A Burst of Light: And Other Essays*. Mineola, NY: Ixia Press.

Lowe, Lisa. 2015. *The Intimacies of Four Continents*. Durham, NC: Duke University Press.

Lowrey, Tom. 2018. 'New Senator Jim Molan Has "No Regrets" about Posting Far-Right Videos on Facebook.' ABC News, 5 February. *https://www.abc. net.au/news/2018-02-05/liberal-senator-jim-molan- shares-anti-muslim-videos/9397246*.

Macdonald, Hamish. 2019. 'How One of Europe's Most Open Countries Closed Its Gates to Immigrants'. ABC News, 8 October. *https://www.abc.net.au/ news/2019-10-08/denmark-the-european-country- turning-its-back-on-immigrants/11574454*.

Magubane, Zine. 2016. 'American Sociology's Racial Ontology: Remembering Slavery, Deconstructing Modernity, and Charting the Future of Global Historical Sociology.' *Cultural Sociology* 10 (3): 369–84.

Malik, Kenan. 2018. 'We're Told 84% of Grooming Gangs Are Asian. But Where's the Evidence?' *The*

Guardian, 11 November. *https://www.theguardian. com/commentisfree/2018/nov/11/84-per-cent-of-grooming-gangs-are-asians-we-dont-know-if-that-figure-is-right.*

Mapping Police Violence. N.d. 'Police Accountability Tool.' *https://mappingpoliceviolence.org/cities.*

May, Theresa. 2016. 'Theresa May's Conference Speech in Full.' *The Telegraph*, 5 October. *https://www.telegraph.co.uk/news/2016/10/05/ theresa-mays-conference-speech-in-full/.*

M'charek, Amade. 2013. 'Beyond Fact or Fiction: On the Materiality of Race in Practice.' *Cultural Anthropology* 28 (3): 420–42.

M'charek, Amade, Katharina Schramm, and David Skinner. 2014. 'Technologies of Belonging: The Absent Presence of Race in Europe.' *Science, Technology, & Human Values* 39 (4): 459–67.

McCormack, Ange. 2016. 'Briggs, Thelma Plum Call out Blackface Photo.' Triple j, 1 February. *https://www.abc.net.au/triplej/programs/hack/ briggs-calls-out-blackface-photo/7129830.*

McDonald, Jessica. 2018. 'The Facts on Elizabeth Warren's DNA Test.' FactCheck.org (blog), 30 October. *https://www.factcheck.org/2018/10/the-facts-on-elizabeth-warrens-dna-test/.*

Mckenzie, Lisa. 2015. 'The Refugee Crisis Will Hit the UK's Working-Class Areas Hardest.' *The Guardian*, 16 September. *https://www. theguardian.com/society/2015/sep/16/refugee-crisis-hit-uk-working-class-powerless.*

Mckenzie, Lisa. 2016. 'Brexit Is the Only Way the Working Class Can Change Anything.' *The Guardian*, 15 June. *https://www.the guardian.com/commentisfree/2016/jun/15/ brexit-working-class-sick-racist-eu-referendum.*

References

Media Diversified. 2018. 'Open Letter: Eugenics Is Back in Vogue Again from the *Observer* to the *Monash Bioethics Review*.' 3 December. *https:// mediadiversified.org/2018/12/03/open-letter-eugenics-is-back-in-vogue-again-from-the-observer-to-the-monash-bioethics-review/.*

Meghji, Ali. 2019. 'Histories of Sociology and Decolonising Education'. *Surviving Society* (podcast). *https://soundcloud.com/user-622675754/e052-ali-meghji-histories-of-sociology-and-decolonising.*

Michallon, Clémence. 2019. 'Liam Neeson Interview: Rape, Race and How I Learnt Revenge Doesn't Work.' *The Independent*, 4 February. *https://www. independent.co.uk/arts-entertainment/films/features/ liam-neeson-interview-rape-race-black-man-revenge-taken-cold-pursuit-a8760896.html.*

Miller, Ryan W. 2019. 'Like Americans, Austrians Are Forgetting the Holocaust. These Are the Shocking Numbers.' *USA Today*, 2 May. *https:// www.usatoday.com/story/news/world/2019/05/02/ austrians-forgetting-holocaust-like-americans-survey-finds/3500048002/.*

Mills, Charles W. 2007. 'White Ignorance.' In *Race and Epistemologies of Ignorance*, edited by Shannon Sullivan and Nancy Tuana. Albany: State University of New York Press.

Mitchell, Peter. 2018. 'I Can't Believe It's Not Samizdat!' *Medium* (blog), 12 November. *https://medium. com/@pdkmitchell/i-can-t-believe-its-not-samizdat-5999145f1c0d?fbclid=IwAR05huqtfYAjamyZhi3Bg FP17KkNTfaFXEKtUU1mWRyl26EK-CgjJaGq0ek.*

Mitropoulos, Angela. 2007. 'On the Borders of the Political – Activism Bound.' *S0metim3s* (blog), 30 June. *https://s0metim3s.com/2007/06/30/on-the-borders-of-the-political/.*

Moisan, Martin. 2019. 'Acte XIV: les pro-Palestiniens qui ont viré Finkielkraut, de faux Gilets jaunes !' *Riposte Laïque*, 16 February. *https:// ripostelaique.com/acte-xiv-les-pro-palestiniens-qui- ont-vire-finkielkraut-de-faux-gilets-jaunes.html*.

Montagu, Ashley. 1962. 'The Concept of Race.' *American Anthropologist* 64 (5): 919–28.

Moreton-Robinson, Aileen. 2015. *The White Possessive: Property, Power, and Indigenous Sovereignty.* Minneapolis: University of Minnesota Press.

Morris, Aldon 2017. *The Scholar Denied: W.E.B. Du Bois and the Birth of Modern Sociology.* Berkeley: University of California Press.

Morsi, Yassir. 2017. *Radical Skin, Moderate Masks: De-Radicalising the Muslim and Racism in Post-Racial Societies.* Lanham, MD: Rowman & Littlefield.

Munier, François. 2014. 'Racisme anti-blanc: texte collectif de militants du MRAP.' Mediapart, 27 January. *https://blogs.mediapart.fr/francois-munier/ blog/270114/racisme-anti-blanc-texte-collectif-de- militants-du-mrap*.

Muñoz, José. 2006. 'Feeling Brown, Feeling Down: Latina Affect, the Performativity of Race, and the Depressive Position.' *Signs* 31 (3): 675–88.

Murray, Douglas. 2019a. 'The False Equivalence of Islamophobia and Anti-Semitism.' *Spectator USA*, 18 March. *https://spectator.us/false-islamophobia- anti-semitism/*.

Murray, Douglas. 2019b. 'Is Cultural Marxism a Myth?' *UnHerd*, 29 March. *https://unherd.com/2019/03/ is-cultural-marxism-a-myth/*.

Nadau, Louis. 2019. 'Alain Finkielkraut répond à ses censeurs "antiracistes": "Le fascisme, c'est vous".' *Marianne*, 24 April. *https://www.marianne.net/*

societe/alain-finkielkraut-repond-ses-censeurs-antira-cistes-le-fascisme-c-est-vous.

Nagle, Angela. 2017. *Kill All Normies: Online Culture Wars from 4chan and Tumblr to Trump and the Alt-Right.* London: Zero Books.

Nagle, Angela. 2018. 'The Left Case Against Open Borders.' *American Affairs Journal* II (4).

New Matilda. 2016. 'Immigration Boss Defends "Nazi Germany" Statement with Fresh Angry Rant.' *New Matilda* (blog), 8 March. *https://newmatilda. com/2016/03/09/immigration-boss-defends-nazi-germany-statement-with-fresh-angry-rant/.*

Nicoll, Fiona. 2004. '"Are You Calling Me a Racist?": Teaching Critical Whiteness Studies in Indigenous Sovereignty.' *Borderlands E-Journal* 3 (2). *http:// www.borderlands.net.au/issues/vol3no2.html.*

O'Brien, Hettie. 2019. 'Wolfgang Streeck: "A Second Referendum Could Tear Society Apart More than the First".' *The New Statesman*, March.

O'Hara, Mary. 2014. 'Zita Holbourne: Fighting Austerity's Bigger Impact on Black and Minority Ethnic People.' *The Guardian*, 5 February. *https:// www.theguardian.com/society/2014/feb/05/ zita-holbourne-barac-austerity-minority-ethnic.*

Olusoga, David. 2019. 'What Does Liam Neeson's "Primal Urge" Really Tell Us about Racism?' *The Guardian*, 9 February. *https://www.theguardian.com/ commentisfree/2019/feb/09/what-does-liam-neeson-primal-urge-tell-us-about-racism.*

Omi, Michael, and Howard Winant. 2013. *Racial Formation in the United States: From the 1960s to the 1990s.* London: Routledge.

Osuna, Steven. 2017. 'Class Suicide: The Black Radical Tradition, Radical Scholarship, and the Neoliberal Turn.' In *The Futures of Black Radicalism*, edited by Gaye Theresa Johnson and Alex Lubin. London: Verso.

Oxman, Michelle. 2018. 'White Feminism, Anti-Semitism, and Intersectionality: We All Have Learning to Do.' *Medium* (blog), 27 November. *https://medium.com/@moxman616_92890/white-feminism-anti-semitism-and-intersectionality-we-all-have-learning-to-do-3c5df6f8f059*.

Palheta, Ugo 2019. 'L'islamophobie en France, une offensive raciste.' *Contretemps: revue de critique communists* (blog), 30 August. *https://www.contretemps.eu/islamophobie-offensive-raciste/*.

Palumbo-Liu, David. 2018. 'France Must Move beyond May 1968 and Tackle the Racial Legacy of Empire.' *The Guardian*, 8 May. *https://www.theguardian.com/commentisfree/2018/may/08/france-may-1968-racial-legacy-empire-50-anniversary*.

Panofsky, Aaron, and Joan Donovan. 2017. 'Genetic Ancestry Testing among White Nationalists.' 17 August. *https://doi.org/10.31235/osf.io/7f9bc*.

Patterson, Orlando. 2018. *Slavery and Social Death: A Comparative Study*. Cambridge MA: Harvard University Press.

Peeples, Lynne. 2019. 'What the Data Say about Police Shootings.' *Nature* 573 (September): 24–6.

Petitjean, Clément, and Étienne Balibar. 2015. 'Étienne Balibar: War, Racism and Nationalism.' Versobooks. com (blog), 17 November. *https://www.versobooks.com/blogs/1559-etienne-balibar-war-racism-and-nationalism*.

Phillips, Melanie. 2019. 'Melanie Phillips: We Must Call Out the Muslims Who Hate Jews.' *The Jewish Chronicle*, 11 April. *https://www.thejc.com/comment/columnists/melanie-phillips-we-must-call-out-the-muslims-who-hate-jews-1.482919*.

Phipps, Alison, and Chantelle Lewis. 2019. 'The *Surviving Society* Alternative to *Woman's Hour*.' *Surviving Society* (podcast). *https://soundcloud.com/user-622675754/e058-the-surviving-society-alternative-to-womans-hour-alison-phipps*.

Pierce, Rebecca. 2019. 'Black Jewish Voices Are Finally Being Heard. So Is The Racist Backlash.' *The Forward*, 24 January. *https://forward.com/opinion/418143/black-jewish-voices-are-finally-being-heard-so-is-the-racist-backlash/*.

Piper, Kira. 2016. 'Leben in Saus und Braus? So Viel Bekommt ein Flüchtling Wirklich.' NTV, 11 May. *https://www.n-tv.de/politik/So-viel-bekommt-ein-Fluechtling-wirklich-article17669556.html*.

Pitcher, Ben. 2006. 'Are You Thinking What We're Thinking? Immigration, Multiculturalism and the Disavowal of Racism in the Run-up to the 2005 British General Election.' *Social Semiotics* 16 (4): 545–51.

Pitt, Bob. 2006. 'Veil Is "an Invitation to Rape" BHL.' Islamophobia Watch, 12 October. *http://www.islamophobiawatch.co.uk/veil-is-an-invitation-to-rape-bhl/*.

Postone, Moishe. 1980. 'Anti-Semitism and National Socialism: Notes on the German Reaction to "Holocaust".' *New German Critique* 19: 97–115.

Povinelli, Elizabeth A. 2007. *The Cunning of Recognition: Indigenous Alterities and the Making of Australian Multiculturalism*. Durham, NC: Duke University Press.

Pulver, Andrew. 2019. 'Liam Neeson Says He Is Not a Racist in Wake of Rape Comments.' *The Guardian*, 5 February. *https://www.theguardian.com/film/2019/feb/05/liam-neeson-says-he-is-not-a-racist-in-wake-of-rape-comments*.

Quijano, Aníbal, and Michael Ennis. 2000. 'Coloniality

of Power, Eurocentrism, and Latin America.' *Nepantla: Views from South* 1 (3): 533–80.

Quillette. 2018. 'Academics' Mobbing of a Young Scholar Must Be Denounced.' *Quillette* (blog), 7 December. *https://quillette.com/2018/12/07/academics-mobbing-of-a-young-scholar-must-be-denounced/*.

Quillette. 2019. 'Against the Militancy of the French "Decolonial" Movement.' *Quillette* (blog), 28 January. *https://quillette.com/2019/01/28/against-the-militancy-of-the-french-decolonial-movement/*.

Razer, Helen. 2018. 'Helen Razer on the Price of No Tomorrow for *Tonightly* … And It's More Than 4 Cents a Day.' *New Matilda* (blog), 6 September. *https://newmatilda.com/2018/09/06/helen-razer-price-no-tomorrow-tonightly-4-cents-day/*.

Reiheld, Alison. 2018. 'A Gimlet Eye: *The Journal of Controversial Ideas* and Jonathan Anomaly's 'Defending Eugenics' (Guest Post).' *Discrimination and Disadvantage*. *https://philosophycommons.typepad.com/disability_and_disadvanta/2018/11/a-gimlet-eye-a-journal-of-controversial-ideas-and-jonathon-anomalys-defending-eugenics.html*.

Reilly, Katie. 2017. Middlebury Has Sanctioned Students for Shutting Down Charles Murray's Lecture.' *Time*, 24 May. *http://time.com/4792694/middlebury-college-discipline-charles-murray-protest/*.

Reynaud-Paligot, Carole. 2009. *La république raciale: paradigme racial et idéologie républicaine (1860–1930)*. Paris: Presses Universitaires de France.

Richmond, Michael, and Alex Charnley. 2017. "The Last Days of a White World.' *Base*, 14 April. *https://www.basepublication.org/?p=452*.

Roberts, Dorothy. 2012. *Fatal Invention: How Science, Politics, and Big Business Re-Create Race in the Twenty-First Century*. New York: The New Press.

References

Roberts, Dorothy. 2015. 'Can Research on the Genetics of Intelligence Be "Socially Neutral"?' *Hastings Center Report* 45 (S1): S50–3.

Robinson, Cedric J. 1983. *Black Marxism: The Making of the Black Radical Tradition*. London: Zed Books.

Roediger, David. 2019a. *Class, Race and Marxism*. London: Verso.

Roediger, David. 2019b. 'White Privilege, White Advantage, White and Human Misery.' Versobooks. com (blog), 8 March. *https://www.versobooks.com/blogs/4262-white-privilege-white-advantage-white-and-human-misery*.

Rojas Weiss, Sabrina. 2019. 'Rep. Alexandria Ocasio-Cortez Calls out Media for Its Weak Description of Steve King.' Yahoo Lifestyle, 13 January. *https://www.yahoo.com/lifestyle/rep-alexandria-ocasio-cortez-calls-media-racially-tinged-description-steve-king-173214010.html*.

Roos, Jerome. 2018. 'From the Demise of Social Democracy to the "End of Capitalism": The Intellectual Trajectory of Wolfgang Streeck.' 29 August. *https://jeromeroos.com/research/intellectual-trajectory-wolfgang-streeck-crisis-social-democracy-end-capitalism*.

Rosenbaum, Martin. 2018. 'Pseudonyms to Protect Authors of Controversial Articles.' BBC News, 12 November. *https://www.bbc.com/news/education-46146766?fbclid=IwAR0S7vhCZWG4xvnfCiHznetQ-0gHGBRD8Z-37TzARdd_cqEBJHJmE9IaFuTs*.

Saucier, P. Khalil, and Tryon P. Woods. 2016. 'Introduction: Racial Optimism and the Drag of Thymotics.' In *Conceptual Aphasia in Black: Displacing Racial Formation*, edited by P. Khalil Saucier and Tryon P. Woods. Lanham, MD: Rowman & Littlefield.

References

SBS. 2016. 'Is Australia Racist?' *https://www.sbs.com.au/ ondemand/video/875663427897/is-australia-racist.*

SBS. 2019. 'Peter Dutton Says IS Brides "Need DNA Testing" to Prove Australian Citizenship.' SBS News, 23 October. *https://www.sbs.com.au/news/ peter-dutton-says-is-brides-need-dna-testing-to-prove-australian-citizenship.*

Schuller, Kyla. 2017. *The Biopolitics of Feeling: Race, Sex, and Science in the Nineteenth Century.* Durham, NC: Duke University Press.

Scroggin, Meredith. 2016. 'Black Lives Matter Began as a Love Letter to Black People.' *The Odyssey Online,* 28 March. *http://theodysseyonline.com/richmond/ lives-matter-others/380575.*

Shaikh, Nermeen, and Gil Anidjar. N.d. 'The Jew, the Arab: An Interview with Gil Anidjar.' Asia Society. *https://asiasociety.org/jew-arab-interview-gil-anidjar.*

Shapiro, Ben. 2019. 'Every Democratic Excuse for Ilhan Omar's Anti-Semitism Is More Vile Than the Last.' *Daily Wire,* 7 March. *https://www.dailywire.com/ news/44380/every-democratic-excuse-ilhan-omars-anti-semitism-ben-shapiro.*

Sharma, Sanjay. 2013. 'Black Twitter? Racial Hashtags, Networks and Contagion.' *New Formations* 78: 46–64.

Sharpe, Christina Elizabeth. 2016. *In the Wake: On Blackness and Being.* Durham, NC: Duke University Press.

Shepherd, Verene. 2015. 'David Cameron, You Still Owe Us for Slavery.' *The Guardian,* 30 September. *https://www.theguardian.com/commentisfree/2015/ sep/30/david-cameron-slavery-caribbean.*

Shilliam, Robbie. 2018a. 'Black/Academia.' In *Decolonising the University,* edited by Gurminder K. Bhambra, Kerem Nisancioglu, and Dalia Gebrial. London: Pluto Press.

References

Shilliam, Robbie. 2018b. *Race and the Undeserving Poor*. Newcastle upon Tyne: Agenda Publishing.

Shim, Janet K. 2014. *Heart-Sick : The Politics of Risk, Inequality, and Heart Disease*. New York: New York University Press.

Singhal, Pallavi. 2019. '"Everything Tarrant Identifies … Is True": Ramsay Centre under Fire for Speakers.' *The Sydney Morning Herald*, 19 March. *https://www.smh.com.au/education/everything-tarrant-identifies-is-true-ramsay-centre-under-fire-for-speakers-20190318-p5157y.html*.

Slabodsky, Santiago. 2015. *Decolonial Judaism: Triumphal Failures of Barbaric Thinking*. New York: Palgrave Macmillan.

Smith, David Norman. 1996. 'The Social Construction of Enemies: Jews and the Representation of Evil.' *Sociological Theory* 14 (3): 203–40.

Smith, Douglas. 2018. 'Far-Right Canadian Duo's Vile Rampage against Aboriginal Culture at Sydney Event.' NITV, 30 July. *https://www.sbs.com.au/nitv/article/2017/07/30/far-right-canadian-duos-vile-rampage-against-aboriginal-culture-sydney-event*.

Smith, Linda Tuhiwai. 2012. *Decolonizing Methodologies: Research and Indigenous Peoples*. London: Zed.

Song, Miri. 2014. 'Challenging a Culture of Racial Equivalence.' *British Journal of Sociology* 65 (1): 107–29.

Soumahoro, Aboubakar. 2019. *Umanità in rivolta: la nostra lotta per il lavoro e il diritto alla felicità*. Milan: Giangiacomo Feltrinelli Editore.

Sparrow, Jeff. 2013. 'Blame the Politicians, Not the Voters.' *Overland Literary Journal* (blog), 19 November. *https://overland.org.au/2013/11/blame-the-politicians-not-the-voters/*.

Sparrow, Jeff. 2018. *Trigger Warnings: Political Correctness and the Rise of the Right*. Brunswick, Vic.: Scribe Publications.

Spillers, Hortense J. 1987. 'Mama's Baby, Papa's Maybe: An American Grammar Book.' *Diacritics* 17 (2): 65–81.

Srilangarajah, Virou. 2018. 'We Are Here Because You Were With Us: Remembering A. Sivanandan (1923–2018).' Versobooks.com (blog), 7 February. *https://www.versobooks.com/blogs/3608-we-are-here-because-you-were-with-us-remembering-a-sivanandan-1923-2018*.

Stoler, Ann Laura. 2002. 'Racial Histories and Their Regimes of Truth.' In *Race Critical Theories*, edited by David Theo Goldberg and Philomena Essed,. London: Blackwell.

Stoler, Ann Laura, and Léopold Lambert. 2014. 'The Colonial Administration of Bodies and Space.' *Archipelago* (podcast), New York. *https://thefunambulist.net/podcast/ann-laura-stoler-the-colonial-administration-of-bodies-and-space*.

Stoneham, Melissa. 2017. 'The Cost of Eating Well in Australia's Remote Indigenous Communities.' *Croakey* (blog), 2017. *https://croakey.org/the-cost-of-eating-well-in-australias-remote-indigenous-communities/*.

Streeck, Wolfgang. 2016a. *Exploding Europe: Germany, the Refugees and the British Vote to Leave*. Vol. 31. SPERI Papers. Sheffield: Sheffield Political Economy Research Institute, University of Sheffield.

Streeck, Wolfgang. 2016b. 'The Post-Capitalist Interregnum: The Old System Is Dying, But a New Social Order Cannot Yet Be Born.' *Juncture* 23 (2): 68–77.

Streeck, Wolfgang. 2017. 'Trump and the Trumpists.' *Inference: International Review of Science* 3 (1). *https://inference-review.com/article/trump-and-the-trumpists*.

References

Streep, Meryl. 2016. 'Setting the Record Straight from Berlin.' *Huffington Post*, 25 February. *https://www. huffpost.com/entry/setting-the-record-straight-from-berlin_b_9310496?guccounter=1*.

Taguieff, Pierre-André. 2002. *La nouvelle judéophobie*. Paris: Fayard – Milles et une nuits.

Tatour, Lana. 2019. 'New Law Old News for Palestinian Apartheid.' *Eureka Street*, 8 February. *https://www.eurekastreet.com.au/article/ new-law-old-news-for-palestinian-apartheid*.

Taylor, Keeanga-Yamahtta. 2016. 'Why Should We Trust You? Clinton's Big Problem with Young Black Americans.' *The Guardian*, 21 October. *https://www.theguardian.com/us-news/2016/oct/21/ hillary-clinton-black-millennial-voters*.

Taylor, Keeanga-Yamahtta. 2019a. 'Black Feminism and the Combahee River Collective.' *Monthly Review* (blog), 1 January. *https://monthlyreview.org/2019/01/01/ black-feminism-and-the-combahee-river-collective/*.

Taylor, Keeanga-Yamahtta. 2019b. 'Five Years Later, Do Black Lives Matter?' *Jacobin*, 30 September. *https://jacobinmag.com/2019/09/black-lives-matter-laquan-mcdonald-mike-brown-eric-garner*.

Taylor, Lenore. 2011. 'Morrison Sees Votes in Anti-Muslim Strategy.' *The Sydney Morning Herald*, 16 February. *https://www.smh.com.au/national/ morrison-sees-votes-in-anti-muslim-strategy-20110216-1awmo.html*.

Terkel, Amanda. 2019. 'Here Are Some of the Death Threats Targeting Rep. Ilhan Omar.' *Huffington Post*, 16 April. *https://www.huffpost.com/entry/ilhan-omar-death-threats-tweets_n_5cb4d7fce4b0ffefe3b50ab3*.

Tietze, Tadeusz. 2014. "Why We Shouldn't Blame Voters for Our Appalling Asylum Policies.' *New Matilda* (blog), 14 July. *https://newmatilda.com/2014/07/14/*

why-we-shouldnt-blame-voters-our-appalling-asylum-policies/.

Titley, Gavan. 2019. *Racism and Media*. London: Sage.

Tooze, Adam. 2017. 'A General Logic of Crisis.' *London Review of Books*, 5 January. *https://www.lrb.co.uk/the-paper/v39/n01/adam-tooze/a-general-logic-of-crisis*.

Topolski, Anya. 2018. 'Good Jew, Bad Jew ... Good Muslim, Bad Muslim: "Managing" Europe's Others.' *Ethnic and Racial Studies* 41 (12): 2179–96.

Traverso, Enzo. 1996. *Pour une critique de la barbarie moderne: écrits sur l'histoire des juifs et de l'antisémitisme*. Lausanne: Éditions Page Deux.

Tuck, Eve, and K. Wayne Yang. 2012. 'Decolonization Is Not a Metaphor.' *Decolonization: Indigeneity, Education & Society* 1 (1): 1–40.

UNESCO. 1968. 'UNESCO Statement on Race and Racial Prejudice'. *Current Anthropology* 9 (4): 270–2.

Usborne, Simon. 2013. 'Revealed: The Third Man in THAT Traditional Britain Photo – and What He Says about the New Loony Right.' *The Independent*, 16 August. *http://www.independent.co.uk/news/uk/politics/revealed-the-third-man-in-that-traditional-britain-photo-and-what-he-says-about-the-new-loony-right-8771448.html*.

van der Merwe, Ben. 2018. 'No, Objecting to Cambridge's Appointment of a Eugenicist Is Not about Free Speech.' *New Statesman*, 20 December. *https://www.newstatesman.com/politics/education/2018/12/no-objecting-cambridge-s-appointment-eugenicist-not-about-free-speech*.

Vincent, Elise. 2012. 'Le "racisme anti-Blancs" divise les antiracistes.' *Le Monde*, 26 October. *https://www.lemonde.fr/societe/article/2012/10/26/le-racisme-anti-blancs-divise-les-antiracistes_1781631_3224.html*.

References

Vitale, Alex. S, and Brian Jordan Jefferson. 2016. 'The Emergence of Command and Control Policing in Neoliberal New York.' In *Policing the Planet: Why the Policing Crisis Led to Black Lives Matter*, edited by Jordan T. Camp and Christina Heatherton. New York: Verso.

Wade, Francis. 2018. 'Ngũgĩ wa Thiong'o and the Tyranny of Language'. *The New York Review of Books*, 6 August. *https://www.nybooks.com/daily/2018/08/06/ngugi-wa-thiongo-and-the-tyranny-of-language/*.

Wahlquist, Calla. 2018. 'Indigenous Children in Care Doubled since Stolen Generations Apology.' *The Guardian*, 25 January. *https://www.theguardian.com/australia-news/2018/jan/25/indigenous-children-in-care-doubled-since-stolen-generations-apology*.

Walters, Suzanna Danuta. 2018. 'In Defense of Identity Politics.' *Signs: Journal of Women in Culture and Society* 43 (2): 473–88.

Wang, Beverley. 2017. 'Whiteness 101: University's Racial Literacy Course Asks Uncomfortable Questions.' ABC News, 5 July. *http://www.abc.net.au/news/2017-07-05/whiteness-uni-racial-literacy-class-asks-uncomfortable-questions/8673994*.

Ward, Victoria, Martin Evans, and Hannah Furness. 2017. 'Who Is Darren Osborne? Everything We Know about the Finsbury Park Mosque Suspect.' *The Daily Telegraph*, 21 June. *http://www.telegraph.co.uk/news/0/darren-osborne-everything-know-finsbury-park-mosque-suspect/*.

Wareham, Sue. 2018. 'Jim Molan, Address the Allegations about Your Time in Iraq.' *New Matilda* (blog), 8 March. *https://newmatilda.com/2018/03/08/jim-molan-address-allegations-time-iraq/*.

Weaver, Matthew, and Peter Walker. 2019. 'Government Sacks Roger Scruton after Remarks about Soros and

Islamophobia.' *The Guardian*, 10 April. *http://www. theguardian.com/culture/2019/apr/10/roger-scruton-calls-for-dismissal-islamophobiad-soros-remarks.*

Weheliye, Alexander. 2014. *Habeas Viscus*. Durham, NC: Duke University Press.

Weisman, Jonathan. 2019. 'American Jews and Israeli Jews Are Headed for a Messy Breakup.' *The New York Times*, 14 January. *https://www.nytimes. com/2019/01/04/opinion/sunday/israeli-jews-american-jews-divide.html.*

Weisskircher, Manès. 2018. 'Will Germans Rise up for a New Left-Wing Movement? What to Know about Aufstehen.' *EUROPP* (blog), 30 August. *https://blogs.lse.ac.uk/europpblog/2018/08/30/ will-germans-rise-up-for-a-new-left-wing-movement-what-to-know-about-aufstehen/.*

Wekker, Gloria. 2016. *White Innocence: Paradoxes of Colonialism and Race*. Durham, NC: Duke University Press.

Wertheim, David J. 2017. *The Jew as Legitimation: Jewish–Gentile Relations beyond Antisemitism and Philosemitism*. New York: Palgrave Macmillan.

West, Cornel. 2017 [1992]. *Race Matters: 25th Anniversary*. Boston: Beacon

White, Ben. 2013. 'Zionists Smear Amnesty over "Cocktail" Joke.' *The Electronic Intifada*, 11 January. *https://electronicintifada.net/blogs/ben-white/ zionists-smear-amnesty-over-cocktail-joke.*

White, Mia. 2019. 'In Defence of Black Sentiment: A Comment on Cedric Johnson's Essay Re: Black Power Nostalgia.' *New Politics* XVII (2). *https://newpol.org/ issue_post/in-defense-of-black-sentiment/.*

Wilderson, Frank. 2016. 'Afro-Pessimism & the End of Redemption.' *The Occupied Times* (blog), 29 March. *https://theoccupiedtimes.org/?p=14236.*

References

Williams, Eric Eustace, and Denis William Brogan. 1964. *Capitalism & Slavery*. London: André Deutsch.

Gilmore, Ruth Wilson. 2006. *Golden Gulag: Prisons, Surplus, Crisis, and Opposition in Globalizing California*. Berkeley: University of California Press.

Wilson, Jason. 2015. '"Cultural Marxism": A Uniting Theory for Rightwingers Who Love to Play the Victim.' *The Guardian*, 19 January. https://www.theguardian.com/commentisfree/2015/jan/19/cultural-marxism-a-uniting-theory-for-rightwingers-who-love-to-play-the-victim.

Wilson, Jason. 2018. '"Dripping with Poison of Antisemitism": The Demonization of George Soros.' *The Guardian*, 25 October. https://www.theguardian.com/us-news/2018/oct/24/george-soros-antisemitism-bomb-attacks.

Winter, Aaron, and Aurelien Mondon. 2019. 'After Christchurch, the Political Class Must Stop Positioning Racism as a Democratic Demand.' Open Democracy, 21 March. https://www.opendemocracy.net/en/opendemocracyuk/after-christchurch-political-class-must-stop-positioning-racism-democratic-demand/.

Wintour, Patrick. 2018. 'Hillary Clinton: Europe Must Curb Immigration to Stop Rightwing Populists.' *The Guardian*, 23 November. https://www.theguardian.com/world/2018/nov/22/hillary-clinton-europe-must-curb-immigration-stop-populists-trump-brexit.

Wolfe, Patrick. 2011. 'Race and the Trace of History: For Henry Reynolds.' In *Studies in Settler Colonialism: Politics, Identity and Culture*, edited by Fiona Bateman and Lionel Pilkington. Houndmills: Palgrave Macmillan.

Wolfe, Patrick. 2016. *Traces of History: Elementary Structures of Race*. London: Verso.

Woodson, C.G. 1950. 'Thomas Jesse Jones.' *The Journal of Negro History* 35 (1): 107–9.

Wynter, Silvia. 1999. 'Towards the Sociogenic Principle: Fanon, the Puzzle of Conscious Experience, of "Identity" and What It's Like to Be "Black".' In *National Identity and Sociopolitical Change: Latin America between Marginizalization and Integration*, edited by Mercedes F. Durán-Cogan and Antonio Gómez-Moriana. University of Minnesota Press.

WYSO. 2018. 'How Can a White Supremacist Be 14 Percent Sub-Saharan African?' WYSO. *https://www. wyso.org/post/how-can-white-supremacist-be-14-percent-sub-saharan-african*.

Yancy, George. 2008. *Black Bodies, White Gazes: The Continuing Significance of Race*. Lanham, MD: Rowman & Littlefield.

Yancy, George. 2015. 'Dear White America.' *Opinionator* (blog), 24 December. *https://opinionator. blogs.nytimes.com/2015/12/24/dear-white-america/*.

Yehuda, Rachel, Amy Lehrner, and Linda M. Bierer. 2018. 'The Public Reception of Putative Epigenetic Mechanisms in the Transgenerational Effects of Trauma.' *Environmental Epigenetics* 4 (2): 1–7.

Yglesias, Matthew. 2018. '*The Bell Curve* Isn't about Science, It's about Policy. And It's Wrong.' *Vox*, 10 April. *https://www.vox.com/2018/4/10/17182692/ bell-curve-charles-murray-policy-wrong*.

Younge, Gary. 2018. 'Ambalavaner Sivanandan Obituary.' *The Guardian*, 7 February. *https://www. theguardian.com/world/2018/feb/07/ambalavaner-sivanandan*.

Younge, Gary. 2019. 'Liam Neeson's Interview Shows That for Some, Black People Are Still Not Fully Human.' *The Guardian*, 5 February. *https://www.*

References

theguardian.com/commentisfree/2019/feb/05/ liam-neeson-interview-black-people-actor-racism.

Zatat, Narjas. 2019. 'Alexandria Ocasio-Cortez Calls Out Reporting of Steve King's "Racist" Remarks.' *The Independent*, 13 January. *https://www.indy100. com/article/alexandria-ocasio-cortez-corrects-reporting-of-steve-king-remarks-racially-tinged-racist-twitter-8725811.*

Zimmerman, Andrew. 2005. 'A German Alabama in Africa: The Tuskegee Expedition to German Togo and the Transnational Origins of West African Cotton Growers.' *The American Historical Review* 110 (5): 1362–98.

Zion, Ilan Ben. 2018. 'Netanyahu Greets Hungary's Orbán as "True Friend of Israel".' AP NEWS, 19 July. *https://apnews.com/938bb193c0894691bf42a6 457d1fae4c.*

Žižek, Slavoj. 2017. *Against the Double Blackmail: Refugees, Terror and Other Troubles with the Neighbours.* London: Penguin.

Zuberi, Tukufu, and Eduardo Bonilla-Silva. 2008. *White Logic, White Methods: Racism and Methodology.* Lanham, MD: Rowman & Littlefield.

Zubovich, Gene. 2016. 'The Strange, Short Career of Judeo-Christianity.' *Aeon*, 22 March. *https://aeon.co/ ideas/the-strange-short-career-of-judeo-christianity.*

Index

231

Index

Index

Index

Index

Index

Index

Index

Index

Index

UNESCO Declaration on Race and Racial Prejudice (1950), 28
United Kingdom
  antisemitism, 61, 133–4
  Brexit, *see* Brexit
  Britain First, 54, 55
  Equality and Human Rights Commission, 61
  Finsbury Park Mosque attack (2017), 62
  Islamophobia, 62, 140–2
  Labour Party, 152–3, 156
  Prevent, 143
  race and class, 173
  racial harassment, 61
United States
  9/11, 144
  1960s social justice movements, 97–8, 99
  2016 presidential elections, 81, 97, 105
  antiracism, 112–18, 123, 126, 130
  antisemitism, 3, 144–5
  Black experiences, 74–7
  Black identity extremism, 130
  Black liberation movement, 110
  border wall, 86
  criminal justice, 115
  El Paso massacre, 1
  heart disease drugs, 40, 41
  identity politics, 111, 112
  internal colonialism, 76–7
  Islamophobia, 143–4, 159
  lantern laws, 8
  lobbyists, 144
  migration, 78, 87
  Native Americans, 29–30
  Obama election, 21, 65
  Occupy movement, 122–3

Pittsburgh Tree of Life synagogue attack (2018), 153–4
  police shootings of Black people, 2
  pro-Israel policies, 143–4
  race and biology, 37
  race discourse, 72
  racism denial, 55
  racism scholarship, 83
  racist terminology, 52–3
  radical politics, 98–9
  red-lining, 83
  settler colonialism, 34
  sickle cell anaemia, 39
  slavery, 8, 44, 48–9, 76, 113
  sociology of race relations, 70, 75–6
  student activism, 99
  Tuskegee syphilis experiment, 39
  see also Trump, Donald
universalism, 12, 73, 84, 96, 110, 128–30
universities, free speech, 22–3
utilitarianism, 22

Vacher de Lapouge, Georges, 69

Wade, Nicholas, 25–6
Walters, Suzanna Danuta, 93
Warren, Elizabeth, 29–30
Washington, Booker T., 76
Weheliye, Alexander, 6, 47, 74, 118–19
Wekker, Gloria, 96, 125
West, Cornel, 12
white genocide, 2, 18, 44–6, 90
white supremacism
  Afropessimism, 118
  biological narratives, 18

241

Index